HAUNTED
INNS AND HOTELS
OF
VIRGINIA

SUSAN SCHWARTZ

Published by Haunted America
A Division of The History Press
Charleston, SC
www.historypress.com

Opposite page, left: Cliff and Gina Middlebrook. *Courtesy of Carolyn Becker. Right*: Carolyn & Eddie Becker.

Unless otherwise indicated, all images are courtesy of the author.

First published 2023

Manufactured in the United States

ISBN 9781467154536

Library of Congress Control Number: 2023934801

Notice: The information in this book is true and complete to the best of our knowledge. It is offered without guarantee on the part of the author or The History Press. The author and The History Press disclaim all liability in connection with the use of this book.

This book was not published or vetted by the Colonial Williamsburg Foundation.

To Cliff & Gina Middlebrook and Carolyn & Eddie Becker: Thanks for all the love and support over the years. We have been through a lot together, and I hope we still get into more mischief in the future. I love you all very much.

CONTENTS

CONTENTS

Acknowledgements

Many individuals contributed to this book and deserve to be recognized for their assistance, as nobody writes a book alone.

The History Press and Haunted America: Thank you so much for this awesome opportunity to share one of my favorite hobbies and take my readers along for the ride. I would also like to send a big thank-you to Kate Jenkins and Rick Delaney for all their assistance with this book. Both were welcoming and didn't mind taking the time to explain how to make things look good throughout the process.

Michael Schwartz: He drove me all over Charlottesville, Harrisonburg, Alexandria and Roanoke to get pictures and interviews. I am grateful for his assistance with all the driving, especially after my major neck surgery. Not only did he help me choose the best pictures to use, but he also took a few of them as well.

Timothy Schwartz: He visited Williamsburg with me and took some awesome pictures, several of which can be found in the following pages. He also helped me edit the finished manuscript and back cover description, always offering great suggestions. In all honesty, I must admit he is a much better writer than I am.

Cliff Middlebrook Jr.: He rode all over Williamsburg and Norfolk with me to visit hotels and inns. I remember one brutal summer day in Colonial Williamsburg when it took both of us to find some of the locations.

Carolyn Becker: She chose some great pictures for the dedication page after we went through a few hundred of them. However, at my son's wedding, she took an even better photo of my brother and his wife.

Catherine Brennan: She edited all the chapters and helped me with questions along the way. Even when my conclusion was downright awful, she still told me it was good. Then, in her infinite wisdom, Cat told me how to make it even better. She is just a really awesome lady who still refuses to rake my leaves for some reason. I am so honored to call her a friend.

Pamela K. Kinney: She sent me information throughout my writing journey on hotels I was researching. She also shared her ghost investigation for the Cavalier Hotel, which I included in all its spooky detail. She has been a wonderful mentor to me, answering all kinds of stupid questions about hauntings, publishing and anything else I can think to ask. You can check Pamela out at her website: https://pamelakkinney.com.

Donald Molnar (Haunted M.D.) and Christine Day: I met Don through a mutual friend, and we hit it off right away. Both of us are in health care and love the paranormal. He gave me loads of information on the Martha Washington Inn and an investigation he and Christine did while staying there. He even shared some pictures with me; one that Christine took even has a ghost in it. He also relayed some of his experiences at the Dunnlora Inn. I appreciate them trusting me to tell their story. If you would like to find out more about Don, you can find him on Facebook, Instagram and YouTube under Haunted M.D.

Maggie O'Brien: She placed me in touch with Sally Bahnsen, who helped me brainstorm my first cover. Thanks so much to this wonderful "pardner!"

Sally Bahnsen: She helped me design the first cover for my book. I am grateful for her assistance in making the cover look more friendly and inviting.

Jacob Floyd (Anubis Press): Jacob, an A+ editor, offered great suggestions on how to improve each section.

Sheri Toney Millikin: She thought I would enjoy a tour of the Dunnlora Inn in Mineral and that it would be a great addition to my book. She was totally correct in her assumption, and I enjoyed visiting the location. She is such a kind lady with a big heart.

Shenia Wong (Dunnlora Inn): She not only warmly welcomed me, but she also regaled me with stories of spooky happenings for most of the morning. I enjoyed my visit and speaking with her about the site and other happenings in town. Discovering a lot of history that I didn't know about the town of Mineral, I went home straightaway to research it some more. She also answered all of my questions and took pictures for me that could be added to the book. She is one awesome lady!

Beth and Betsy (Richard Johnston Inn): These two sweet ladies gave me an impromptu but informative tour of the inn and told me a few ghost stories along the way. Their hospitality was impeccable.

Michelle (Black Horse Inn): This sweet chef told me some stories and answered my questions before pointing me in the direction of the stairs to see if I could capture anything myself. I was thankful to have someone so welcoming to tell me about the inn.

Josh (Natural Bridge Hotel): I met Josh when I stopped at the Natural Bridge Hotel to ask about the hauntings there. He told me some history behind the hotel and then explained some hauntings at the Hotel Roanoke. I enjoyed his tales of ghostly happenings at each location.

Michelle Darnell (Belle Grove Plantation Bed & Breakfast): Michelle was very excited to have me take a tour with her. Unfortunately, COVID came without warning, and I never had a chance to visit before everyone was ordered to stay home. I am planning to go as soon as I can, because this property sounds absolutely incredible. Her haunting tales of the Lady in White, Jacob and the Caretaker make me want to check out the location even more. She even has two ghost kitties that I hope to both see and hear when I visit.

Shawna (Olde Towne Inn): Shawna, the manager, was accommodating when I visited and asked about the current haunting with Miss Lucy. I am thankful she took time to answer all my questions.

The readers: You are the most important ones here. I thank you so much for reading my book, and I hope you do get to visit some of the wonderful places described in its pages. Have fun and be safe!

Please note: Do not venture onto anyone's property without their express permission. Always call ahead and ask first.

INTRODUCTION

While traveling and researching for this book, I discovered that many locations have between one and ten (or more) ghosts. Some sites are very active, while others aren't. It depends on the history, location and time of year.

I don't take much when I go to a haunted location, just my camera and an audio recorder for electronic voice phenomenon (EVP). Other equipment that can be employed to investigate haunted locations are the following: EMF meters, K2 meters, parascopes, REM pods, an ovilus (spirit box) and movement sensors.

All of these will facilitate a great ghost-hunting experience, but the main goal is to have fun and see what you get. Remember, spirits don't always cooperate when you want them to do something. Patience will take you far in this field. The most important rule by far is *never* go ghost hunting alone. Anything can happen! Please be safe when visiting any location.

I have visited most of these locations, but there are some that I didn't get to investigate, as many of the rooms involved in the hauntings had guests staying in them at the time. While that was a small setback, I still encourage you to visit and let these stories come alive for you. (Note: Don't ever bother guests staying in specific rooms.)

I had so much fun researching this book and enjoyed visiting each location that was open to exploring. Some of the locations have closed since I first visited them, but I hope you will still visit and see what you get in the way of pictures and recordings. I placed the locations in a specific order in this book, as I did for *Haunted Charlottesville and Surrounding Counties*. This arrangement of the sites allows a visitor to see many on the same day or to start by investigating a favorite location. I have added some other haunted and odd locations and ghost tours to pique your interest even more.

I hope you will visit some of these places, maybe even spend the night. Perhaps you will discover an extra guest you don't recall having brought with you.

1

Tidewater & Virginia Beach

Cavalier Hotel

After a four-year period of restoration, the Cavalier Hotel reopened its beachfront doors in March 2018. Boasting 195 guest rooms in the original building, its opening in 1927 added a major source of development to the area. Most of the suites had a gorgeous view of the Atlantic Ocean. In 1942, it was employed by the U.S. Navy as a training center, quickly facilitating those soldiers joining World War II.

Many famous guests stayed at the Cavalier Hotel, including Will Rogers, Fatty Arbuckle, Bette Davis, Judy Garland, F. Scott Fitzgerald, Bob Hope, Frank Sinatra and Bing Crosby. Presidents also enjoyed the comforts of this fine establishment, starting with Calvin Coolidge (1923–29) and continuing to Jimmy Carter (1977–81).

Guests at the hotel tell of a soldier in army uniform who continually warns visitors not to wander to the upper floors, because "there are so many bodies up there." It was discovered that several bodies had washed ashore after a nearby ship blew up at sea.

Adolph Coors, who started Coors Brewing Company, jumped from the sixth floor to his death in 1929. Some say he was pushed. But, being eighty at the time, he could have just lost his balance. When walking past the exact place where Coors hit the ground, some guests say they hear a loud thud.

Cavalier Hotel.

When local author Al Chewning conducts ghost tours, he discusses the property. He begins by holding up a picture of Adolph Coors and telling a story about photos taken during a wedding at the hotel in the 1970s. A woman who attended the wedding saw an older gentleman in some of the pictures, but no one knew who he was. Years later, when Chewning held the picture of Coors up during a tour, a woman screamed. She had attended that wedding years before, and the man in the picture looked just like the unidentified gentleman. Apparently, Coors decided to make sure his beverages were being used at the wedding.

On a weird and personal note, while I was talking with my husband, Michael, about some of the wording in the paragraphs above, he asked what Coors looked like—creepy or distinguished? About the time Michael said "creepy," the contents of the bottom cabinet—pots, pans and other cookware—came crashing out onto the floor. I quickly told told him not to ever say Coors was creepy, because he probably didn't like that.

Several peculiar things happen at this hotel, such as the elevators running when no one is riding in them. Some guests complain of their towels changing color when they leave the room. There are feelings of being watched in the hallways and in the Pocahontas and Hunt Rooms. A server in the restaurant and bar area walks through walls. Toilets will flush without being used. The Pocahontas Room, known as the Becca Restaurant to honor Pocahontas's English name, Rebecca, has a woman that shows up frequently with her dog.

A good friend and fellow author, Pamela K. Kinney, spent two nights at the hotel and managed to do some investigating. After going through pictures she had snapped in the pool room, she found that one had the outline of a person near the fallout shelter sign. Venturing out for dinner one night, Pamela ran into a plumber fixing some pipes. He complained about kids running around on the floor above them. There were no kids in the hotel at the time.

After dinner, Pamela retired for the evening to Room 466. She awoke in the middle of the night to find a gentleman in a suit standing over her. The man sat down on the foot of the bed, which caused Pamela to sit straight up, after which he simply vanished. She also discovered that a fake red rose petal had fallen under her bed. (The Cavalier had hosted a Valentine's Day party, and these rose petals were all over the floors of the hotel.) The next day, it was missing from a zipped-up bag in her purse. She also felt someone playing with her hair for part of the night. She did discover that the person staying in Room 366 also had some issues, particularly with their computer. The device's alarm kept going off, so the guest unplugged it from the wall to stop the noise, but the computer kept beeping on its own.

Before departing the Cavalier, Pamela thought she would try one more investigation starting on the sixth floor. Nothing happened, so she went down to the fifth floor to take some recordings and pictures. Stepping out of the elevator, Pamela inquired if anyone had anything to say. She heard a resounding "no," with the voice sounding like it was right beside her. She also heard it on the recording when she got home.

Apparently, a little girl once lost her cat at the hotel and went to look for it by herself. The cat had fallen in the hotel's pool, and the girl tried to save it and wound up drowning with the animal. Many guests hear a cat meowing and scratching at their doors, only to find there are no cats on the property. The noises are heard near the pool as well, and they are accompanied by the sounds of a small child. Small catlike footprints have been seen in one of the back stairwells. Some workers say they have felt the weight of a cat lying on their workspace or paperwork. If they fool with the spirit animal, it has been known to scratch them in irritation. The bartenders have celebrated the life of the kitty by naming a drink Ghost Cat.

The Historic Cavalier Hotel
4200 Atlantic Avenue
Virginia Beach, VA 23451
757-425-8555
https://cavalierresortvb.com/cavalier-hotel

GLENCOE INN

This charming bed-and-breakfast has a great view from the verandah overlooking the Elizabeth River. Built in 1890, the gorgeous inn is located in the heart of downtown Portsmouth, and it encompasses many influences of the original owner's Scottish lifestyle, such as homemade scones.

There is one spirit who decided to stay at the Glencoe permanently. Many guests have seen an elderly woman, roughly in her eighties, tending to her rose garden. Whenever she visits the inn, a strong scent of roses is detected. This happens frequently in the winter months, when there are no roses for her to tend.

For another interesting site, head down to the Grice-Neely House at 202 North Street, located at the other end of the block. (https://thebackyardexplorer.wordpress.com/2012/08/30/grice-neely-house-202-north-street). On the side closest to the intersection, take a look at the lone step leading to the next level. It is a large tombstone. Although the location is not a hotel, it is reportedly haunted by an enslaved person, who has

Glencoe Inn.

Tombstone step at Grice-Neely House.

appeared to witnesses staying in the home. To those who have seen him, they say he appears very confused. A medium once told the occupants to board up the back window after the next person died in the house. It was hoped that this would stop the hauntings. Sadly, it did not.

Glencoe Inn
222 North Street
Portsmouth, VA 23704
757-397-8128
http://www.glencoeinn.com

Page House Inn

Located in historic Ghent, this spacious inn offers seven rooms filled with gorgeous decor and claw-foot tubs. With its charm and elegance, this bed-and-breakfast is filled with amenities and a great atmosphere. The innkeeper, Debbie, along with her sweet dog, Frankie, is available to welcome guests and keep them comfortable during their stay.

Herman and Adella Page, along with their four children, built this house in 1899. One of the Page sons even worked as the first postmaster general in Norfolk.

Former owner Stephanie Dibelardino believes that her mother, Jean Martino, loved the place so much that she has yet to leave. Jean died before Stephanie opened the inn in 1998, and it is believed that she is the one haunting the location. Jean's favorite china cabinet still remains in the inn, and its doors often open and close by themselves. Unexplained voices and footsteps are heard throughout the house. When the areas are checked, no one is found. Is Jean still watching over her beloved china and the guests who stay at the Page House Inn?

Page House Inn (closed in 2021)
323 Fairfax Avenue
Norfolk, VA 23507
757-625-5033

Page House Inn.

MANSION ON MAIN BED & BREAKFAST

Known as the Thomas House back in 1889, this Smithfield mansion sits at the corner of Main and Church Streets atop Wharf Hill, where a thriving seaport used to be located. Richard and Frances Thomas built the beautiful home, incorporating marble fireplaces and pinewood flooring, in the historic district. Richard was the town historian and a prominent lawyer at the time.

Mansion-on-Main Bed & Breakfast.

The mansion remained a private residence for many years. But in 1995, Sala Clark decided to restore the property and make it into a bed-and-breakfast. She discovered in her research that before the turn of the century, the house was known as the Mansion on Main. It has been called that ever since. Sadly, Sala passed away before renovations could be completed. Her mother, Betty Clark, owns the mansion as well as a small antiques shop behind the bed-and-breakfast. The business offers tours, and you can stay overnight and enjoy a traditional southern breakfast.

The manager of the property, Dawn Riddle, has said in many interviews that the mansion is not haunted. Sweet spirits, however, are allowed. My son, Timothy, filmed an episode of the television show *A Haunting* there. The episode, "Haunted Victorian," made the mansion look very spooky in some scenes, especially with the furniture covered in sheets and with low lighting and black-and-white pictures on the walls.

Timothy took me to see the house while driving in the Smithfield area. Turning a corner, there stood the mansion in all its splendor. I thought it was definitely haunted, and if it wasn't, the ghosts were missing out on a great place. Timothy said this was where filming had taken place for the episode. He said nothing much happened during the shoot, but they did hear voices they couldn't explain, and objects were moved around the set by unseen hands.

Mansion on Main Bed & Breakfast
36 Main Street
Smithfield, VA 23430
757-357-0006
https://www.mansion-on-main.com

THE CHAMBERLIN / FORT MONROE

This delightful retirement home was once a bustling hotel. The Chamberlin replaced the Hygeia (first version, 1820, second version, 1863), which was torn down after the hotel served as a Civil War hospital. Constructed in 1927, the Chamberlin, located inside Fort Monroe, offers breathtaking views of the Chesapeake Bay from its main dining area at the water. Edgar Allan Poe recited his famous poem *The Raven* here before he died in Maryland in 1849. There is a museum located behind the gift shop housing mementoes from the history of the Chamberlin.

Many hauntings have occurred at the location. Perhaps the most famous is of a young woman named Ezmerelda, who is waiting for her father to return from a fishing trip. She plays a tune on their piano and knocks objects off of shelves. A teenage girl who died in a fire on the seventh floor can be heard banging on the walls and seen looking out the windows. Described as having long brown hair and dressed in white clothing, she is sometimes seen in the windows of the storage rooms on the fort.

Down the road, located around the site of the former hotel, Fort Monroe at 30 Ingalls Road is also haunted (https://www.nps.gov/fomr/index.htm). Known as one of the largest fortifications made of stone in America, it controlled all business from the York and James Rivers in the area. Founded by John Smith in 1608 and named after the fifth U.S. president, James Monroe, this fort was once known as Old Point Comfort. Amazingly, some researchers think that some oak trees on the site were living during that time. It is also one of a few forts never captured by the Confederate army during the Civil War.

Many visitors have seen or felt something as they explore the former Civil War base. The buildings beyond the moat are especially active. People might feel a pinch or a poke, and apparitions in Civil War dress can be seen and heard.

Jefferson Davis loved to take walks in the evening after being imprisoned for plotting to kill Abraham Lincoln. His wife, ever vigilant, kept an eye on him to make sure he made it back safely. If you go in the evening, watch for Davis walking through the streets and his wife looking after him from afar. Davis also haunts the cell where he was incarcerated on the base, Casemate No. 2.

Quarters No. 1 is the site of several hauntings by Abraham Lincoln, who spent four nights there. There have also been recordings of a little girl searching for her cat and of unexplained voices, and several pictures that

The Chamberlin.

visitors have taken have orbs in them. Visitors have also seen Ulysses S. Grant roaming the location.

A former resident told of one evening when she found a man standing in her dining room, propped up against the mantel and dressed in eighteenth-century clothing. He vanished suddenly with no explanation. Her son saw a strange mist hovering in his bedroom as well.

The Old Point Comfort Lighthouse, built in 1862 and still in use today, has had its share of spooky visitors. These include Captain John Smith, Abraham Lincoln, Jefferson Davis and unidentified ghostly figures.

Behind the lighthouse, a huge moat is seen. It is said that a sea serpent of some sort lurks in the waters. The creature has been sighted several times, but no one can identify what it is exactly. Robert E. Lee was responsible for excavating the land and developing the moat at the location.

Many have claimed to see a small boy in the house beside the moat wall. He haunts the upstairs, causing mischief.

Another ghost roaming the base is a woman in a white dress. She is sometimes seen at the boardwalk and near a well-known area called "Ghost Alley," or Matthew Lane. Camille Kirtz married a captain who was much older and whose position required that he travel extensively. His wife began seeing a French captain the same age as her. They quickly fell in love. One night, the husband came home to find them in bed. He chased the other man out of their home, returned and murdered his wife. It is also said that he may have been trying to shoot the Frenchman and hit his wife instead. Her ghost is said to be still looking for her lost love.

Left: Old Point Comfort Lighthouse.

Below: Fort Monroe Moat.

Edgar Allan Poe also wanders through the No. 5 Barracks building. He lived there while on base and returned to present some poetry about a month before he died in Baltimore.

Another location in Ghost Alley is said to have an entity that cannot stand roses. If a vase is placed in one of the homes, the roses will be thrown on the floor after some time. It is thought to be a scorned lover upset over her lost love.

The Chamberlin
2 Fenwick Road
Hampton, VA 23651
757-506-0833
The Chamberlin: https://www.agewellliving.com/senior-living/va/hampton/the-chamberlin

HISTORIC BOXWOOD INN

Built in 1897, this southern home once belonged to Simon Curtis, who was "Boss Man" of Warwick County, serving as county treasurer, road commissioner and postmaster. It was designed to allow for other types of businesses, and Curtis added rooms for his family and a general store complete with a post office, a tax assessor's office and a Hall of Records. The family had a grand time hosting parties for political events or just renting out the rooms to soldiers returning from war.

Coleman Curtis, the oldest son, lived in the home after his parents died in the 1940s. His wife, Edith, joined him and brought her collection of antiques to decorate her new home.

The house was set to be destroyed, but the Lucas family bought and restored it in 1995, renaming it the Boxwood Inn. The location was added to the Virginia Landmarks Register. Mrs. Lucas walked downstairs one day, saying she needed a nail file. She suddenly spotted one out in the open. This pleased her so much that she next asked for $100. A few minutes later, there was something stuck to the bottom of one of her shoes. It was a gold tooth that turned out to be worth $100. Mrs. Lucas always thought Nannie Curtis was the purveyor of this goodwill throughout the history of the inn.

Kathy Hulick, the owner since 2008, says she didn't believe in ghosts until she purchased the inn. She has experienced many strange occurrences,

Historic Boxwood Inn.

such as marching sounds from empty rooms and someone pulling her hair or the back of her shirt. She often finds her silverware rearranged in the dining room.

The magnificent mansion is said to have at least twelve spirits. One is thought to be Nannie Curtis. She likes to open and close doors as well as knock on them in the early morning. Another spirit is an older gentleman who carries a cane and appears to guests only at certain times. Several others are thought to be men who helped build the mansion.

Historic Boxwood Inn
10 Elmhurst Street
Newport News, VA 23603
757-735-1112
https://historicboxwoodinn.com

2
WILLIAMSBURG & CHARLES CITY

CHISWELL–BUCKTROUT HOUSE AND KITCHEN

Although many house records were destroyed during the Civil War, it is believed that the Chiswell-Bucktrout House was completed in 1764. Colonel John Chiswell lived in the home until 1766, when he was accused of murder. He ran a sword through Robert Routledge, a supposed friend. Chiswell was charged but died in his home under mysterious circumstances before the trial. After Chiswell's death, a renowned cabinetmaker from London named Benjamin Bucktrout purchased the home.

Many guests say they have been touched by a spirit while sleeping or moving through the house. Many cold spots have been noted, as well as disembodied voices, whispering and a scent of tobacco that cannot be explained. Other occurrences include clothes falling off hangers, moving items and unexplained footsteps. A man decided to stay in one of the kitchen rooms, which are separated from the main building and other guest rooms. Used as an old slave kitchen, this building now contains several guest rooms. The man awoke one night around 4:00 a.m. to find a shaking black cloud hovering over him. When he took a swipe at it, it disappeared. He and his wife stayed up with the lights on the rest of the night. The next morning, when they asked for a room change, the manager didn't seem surprised at their story. He stated that some things just cannot be explained.

Chiswell-Bucktrout House and Kitchen. *Courtesy of Timothy Schwartz.*

The ghost is thought to be the colonel himself. His death was sudden and unexpected, leading some to believe he committed suicide. There are no records to verify this claim. We can only hope that he finally finds peace in the afterlife.

Chiswell-Bucktrout House and Kitchen
416 East Francis Street
Williamsburg, VA 23185
For reservations: 855-231-7240
https://www.colonialwilliamsburghotels.com/accommodations/
historic-lodging

ORRELL HOUSE

Giving guests and visitors a taste of life in the eighteenth century, the Orrell House is one of the oldest structures in Colonial Williamsburg. Possibly built in the 1750s, the house was named after John Orrell, who lived there for almost twenty years. Today, even though the furniture throughout the building is from a different era, modern amenities, such as television and air-conditioning, are available to make today's weary traveler feel more comfortable. There is a kitchen attachment in the yellow house, which is to the side of the main building. Kitchens were placed in an attached structure, as people were afraid kitchen fires would burn other structures if embers flew the wrong way.

Mysterious occurrences happening in the house give weight to the haunted stories. One family heard running water one night, and the husband went to investigate the cause. The bathroom sink had been left

Orrell House.

on, so he shut it off and went back to watching TV with his family. The faucet somehow turned on again without anyone going near it.

Another family heard the sound of breaking glass late one night. They found a glass in the bathroom shattered on the floor. The next morning, the bathroom was covered in toilet paper from top to bottom. In addition, when guests go out to dinner, they often return to find all the furniture turned upside down.

Orrell House
302 East Francis Street
Williamsburg, VA 23185
757-565-8440/855-231-7240
https://www.colonialwilliamsburghotels.com/accommodations/
historic-lodging/

BRACKEN TENEMENT KITCHEN

Located on East Francis Street, this kitchen, like many others, is detached from the main house. This prevented the spread of fire and malodorous scents from the kitchen into the house. Construction started in 1928, when all of Colonial Williamsburg went through a restoration phase. After the first phase, Williamsburg became popular when Franklin Roosevelt visited and officially opened Duke of Gloucester Street. Finding out the original owners of this site has been difficult, between the wars and the fires taking place from the 1700s to the present day.

Some accounts of hauntings seem to share the same aspect: a woman in a dark dress in a rocking chair downstairs. Many say they have seen the chair rock when no one is sitting in it. The woman, when seen, seems to watch passersby traveling down the road.

Bracken Tenement Kitchen
206 East Francis Street
Williamsburg, VA 23185
888-965-7254
https://www.colonialwilliamsburg.org/locations/the-bracken-kitchen

Bracken Tenement Kitchen.

LIGHTFOOT HOUSE

Lightfoot House, one of the original eighty-eight buildings from the colonial era, is still standing in Williamsburg today. From 1740 to 1838, the Lightfoot family lived in the home while leasing out the land around them. William Peachy, who also owned the Peyton Randolph House, was a tenant of the Lightfoot family. Today, the house is known for its unique architecture and is offered to heads of state, foreign dignitaries and celebrities for their stay in Williamsburg.

The main staff reports paranormal activity on a regular basis. Maids see men dressed in colonial period clothing walking down the hall. Sometimes, after making the beds in some rooms, they will check that everything is completed and find the bed has been stripped of its sheets. Objects placed on shelves will disappear and turn up in other spots.

Lightfoot House. *Courtesy of Timothy Schwartz.*

Lightfoot House
114 East Francis Street
Williamsburg, VA 23185
855-231-7240
https://www.colonialwilliamsburghotels.com/accommodations/historic-lodging

MARKET SQUARE TAVERN AND KITCHEN

Market Square Tavern is another of Colonial Williamsburg's eighty-eight original buildings. Boasting eleven rooms, it has been in operation since 1749. John Dixon originally owned the tavern. After it exchanged hands many times, Robert Lyon took over as manager. This was about the time Thomas Jefferson was in residence. A fire broke out in 1842 and damaged the tavern and several of the side buildings. After the tavern was rebuilt, it was named the Raleigh Tavern, which later became the Raleigh Hotel.

Market Square Tavern.

During the Civil War, a church sat beside the Raleigh called the Greek Revival Church, which was also lost in the aforementioned fire. It was used as a hospital; soldiers suffered amputations and death at the location. There are more than two hundred bodies buried in a mass grave near the church. Spirits of the soldiers are seen walking the site. If you listen closely, you might still hear their screams of pain and anguish.

Thomas Jefferson lived at the tavern while he attended the College of William & Mary, and many have seen his ghost at the location. One guest heard a noise in the hallway that sounded like someone pacing, so he called out, "Goodnight, Tom!" He then heard a chair scraping backward, as if someone was getting up to leave.

Other strange incidents have occurred, such as tapping on the walls and seeing people in colonial garb walking through the halls. When a guest walks up to them, they disappear.

Market Square Tavern and Kitchen
110 East Duke of Gloucester Street
Williamsburg, VA 23185
855-231-7240
https://www.colonialwilliamsburghotels.com/accommodations/
historic-lodging

KING'S ARMS TAVERN

For another haunted experience, travel down the street a little ways to this authentic colonial tavern. Jane Vobe opened the King's Arms Tavern in February 1772, catering to politicians and government employees. As a result, two of her favorite guests were George Washington and Thomas Jefferson, the first and third presidents of the United States, respectively.

The colonists would meet here to enjoy music and great food. Hunters' Game Pye is an authentic colonial dish served at the tavern. It is a mix of duck, rabbit and venison with some bacon and vegetables thrown into a flaky crust. The tavern also serves steak and pork dishes for those who like a more traditional meal.

The hauntings at the tavern are said to be caused by a ghost named Irma. Irma not only worked at the tavern but also died there in a fire caused by a dropped candle. Some say she died of a heart attack in her bedroom upstairs in the 1950s. She is a friendly and helpful spirit, and the staff wishes her a good night before leaving for the night.

Irma usually appears only to the tavern employees. She has been seen in colonial dress walking through doors and as a reflection in a mirror, only to have employees turn around to find nobody standing behind them. Windows lock and unlock on their own, and candles are blown out despite

King's Arms Tavern. *Courtesy of Timothy Schwartz.*

being surrounded by glass. Reports of menus falling out of drawers and trays toppling over are normal occurrences at the tavern.

King's Arms Tavern
416 East Duke of Gloucester Street
Williamsburg, VA 23185
855-578-0080
855-231-7240
https://www.colonialwilliamsburghotels.com/accommodations/
historic-lodging

BRICK HOUSE TAVERN

Opened in 1770 by Mary Davis, Brick House Tavern is an alternative to traditional lodging in Colonial Williamsburg. It is located down from the Colonial Williamsburg Bindery and across from the William Pitt Store. Though the present building is not the original, it stands on the original site. The tavern contains sixteen guest rooms on two floors. When the establishment first opened, Davis decreed that the first-floor rooms

would be for women and those on the second floor for men. Guests paid for a room, but it wouldn't necessarily be a "private room." They would have their own bed, but other people, possibly strangers, would share the room with them.

The Brick House has its share of hauntings. Some visitors hear keys being jangled and footsteps stomping down the hallways. Some have seen shadowy figures

Brick House Tavern. *Courtesy of Timothy Schwartz.*

roaming the halls; others have had the lights in their rooms turned off and on at different intervals. Complaints of a tobacco smell have been noted, which is strange, because the whole building is smoke-free. One female guest awoke to a man in breeches trying to kiss her. Other guests trying to get a good night's sleep complain of their covers being pulled off and of being pressed down into the bed by their shoulders.

Brick House Tavern
300–398 East Duke of Gloucester Street
Williamsburg, VA 23185
888-965-7254
https://www.colonialwilliamsburg.org/locations/brick-house-shop

NORTH BEND PLANTATION

Once occupied by the Weanoc Indians, the land passed down to John Minge, who in 1801 constructed the Federal Greek Revival–style home for his wife, Sarah Harrison. The main house still stands on the 850-acre property. The house is now owned by George Copland III, descendant of William Henry Harrison, Sarah's brother and the ninth U.S. president. George left many of the original structures as they were, including the dairy house, smokehouse and icehouse. Inside the house are such treasures as family china, rare books, antiques and family heirlooms, as well as a collection of old dolls.

In 1864, Thomas Wilcox, the owner of the plantation, left to stay at Belle Air Plantation, as more than thirty thousand troops from the Union started to camp out on his property. Led by General Philip Sheridan, the Union army worked on building a bridge across the James River. General Sheridan's desk can still be found at North Bend today.

There have been many reports of ghostly visitors here over the years. Footsteps and pacing have been heard by the Coplands on several occasions. Ms. Copland heard what she thought was someone wearing boots stomp across the floor. She called her son to investigate, but no one was ever found in the rooms with the sounds. Her son decided to stay the night, but nothing occurred. The family seems to think General Sheridan has come back to reflect on what he could have done better in the war. Another couple who stayed said they felt the presence of evil, so the man said a

North Bend Plantation.

short prayer of protection. He then heard what sounded like a young child crying as if being hurt. The gentleman also said that something pushed him, so he gave the spirit a hard shove back. The couple left at first light.

North Bend Plantation
12200 Weyanoke Road
Charles City, Virginia 23030
804-829-5176
http://www.northbendplantation.com

Edgewood Plantation

Located about thirty miles from Williamsburg, Virginia, Edgewood Plantation is a quaint bed-and-breakfast that features a double winding staircase, a stunning interior and eight opulent guest rooms. Outside, there is an in-ground pool along with two gazebos where guests can enjoy the sounds of nature. Bicyclists will often stop here to pitch a tent or get a refreshing cold drink before continuing their journey.

Edgewood Plantation's location was a strategic one during two historic wars. Rowland's Mill became the headquarters of Benedict Arnold during the American Revolution. During the Civil War, corn from the mill fed the hardworking men, and Confederate soldiers found it easy to spy on Union General George McClellan's troops, who were camping in the next field. Westover Episcopal even offered Sunday services for those present. The site was also used as a war hospital. The Rowlands, who acquired the property in the 1840s, remembered seeing wagons filled with the wounded and dead. This could be one explanation for the many ghosts seen at the plantation.

Once an ancestral home to William Henry and Benjamin Harrison, Edgewood Plantation used to be a section of Berkeley Plantation. The house has been the site of many different businesses, including a restaurant, a church, a nursing home and a post office. The third floor of the building was used as a lookout station by Confederate generals watching out for attacks along Route 5 (John Tyler Memorial Highway), which is also one of the oldest roads in the United States. It is said that J.E.B. Stuart even stopped at the plantation long enough to get some coffee on his way to meet General Robert E. Lee in Richmond to alert him about the strength the Union army would be bringing.

Benjamin Harrison V bought some 22,000 acres, which he turned into the Berkeley Plantation in 1726. In 1840, Spencer Rowland and his family traveled from New Jersey to purchase the corn mill, along with 1,800 acres of property. Spencer Rowland completed Edgewood in 1849.

Edgewood Plantation.

Spencer's daughter Elizabeth was also known as Lizzie. Many guests have seen her face peering at them from a second-floor bedroom. It is surmised that, since her name was etched into one of the windows, the room must have belonged to her. Lizzie's lover went off to fight in the war and never returned. She still stands at the window, awaiting his return. Lizzie passed away at age forty-seven in 1870 of a broken heart. The home stayed in the Rowland family until 1888. It then passed through many owners until the current family bought the property.

Lizzie likes to play tricks on the current owners, Dot and Julian Boulware. They hear knocks they can't explain, noises from empty rooms and footsteps up and down the staircase, and they see lights flicker by themselves. Dot hosted a dinner party in 1978, and all the guests wanted to know more about Lizzie, except one lady, who swore she didn't believe in ghosts. Just then, a brass plate on a shelf behind the lady flew off and hit her on the shoulder.

One night, the house experienced a terrible storm and lost all electricity. It was completely dark, as the home had no kerosene lamps lit. All of a sudden, the guests awoke to someone ascending the stairs. They began to call out one another's names but received no answer. Julian grabbed his gun and went to investigate. Dot told him it was probably Lizzie acting up again. They both went downstairs and walked through the house but found no one who could have made the noise.

The slave quarters are known to be very haunted. A ghost cat is said to have caused some uproar when a ghost-hunting team came to investigate with electromagnetic equipment and voice detectors. Along with these hauntings, several others have been noted. Two suicides also lend to the lore at Edgewood. An elderly fellow apparently killed himself in the mill, and a female was found hanging from the stairs in the house. Could she be the one people hear walking up the stairs at night?

Luckily, Edgewood Plantation will be around for many years. Being in the National Register of Historic Places, the house provides a link to both the site's history and some of the dead who may still be wandering the property.

Edgewood Plantation
4800 John Tyler Memorial Highway
Charles City, VA 23030
804-829-2962
https://www.edgewoodplantation.com

3

RICHMOND & MINERAL

LINDEN ROW INN

Linden Row Inn is located in downtown Richmond near First and Franklin Streets. Designed with a European flair, the inn consists of Greek Revival houses built in the mid-nineteenth century. Charles Ellis purchased the land in 1816. His children and their friend Edgar Allan Poe (1809–1849) would play in the gardens each day. As Poe grew into adolescence, he returned to these gardens many times, and it was thought that he wrote one of his poems, "To Helen," and one of his short stories, "The Domain of Arnheim," there. In his poem "To One in Paradise," Poe describes the beautiful gardens surrounding the property where two lovers once met. This mirrors Poe's life, as it was in these gardens that Poe met his future fiancée, Elmira Royster. The location is listed in the National Register of Historic Places.

The area became a gathering spot for military leaders in the Civil War, especially Virginia Pegram's parlor, which is Suite 220. Her daughter Mary opened the Southern Female Institute two doors down from the family home. Another school in Linden Row also educated many women, including the first woman to serve in the House of Commons in England.

After several houses were demolished to make way for new homes and businesses on the busy street, Mary Wingfield Scott bought seven of the homes in the 1950s to preserve a piece of history. After the properties were donated to the Historic Richmond Foundation, Scott guaranteed the property would be maintained. It became a seventy-room inn in 1988 with an accompanying garden and carriage houses.

As far as hauntings go, most guests who stay in the Parlor Suites say they feel as if Poe was hanging out with them in the outside garden. Perhaps he is still using the scenery as inspiration for his writing. For true fans of the writer, the Poe Museum is a short drive from Linden Row. It is plenty haunted, too.

For the staff, there are a few entities that seem to lurk in the long hallways. One staff member said that one room is unique, in that people who stay there usually leave quickly due to eerie feelings they experience. There are also rooms on the third and fourth floors that staff members don't like to enter. They speak of a special "something" that might rip your covers off, turn the TV on and off and rattle doorknobs late at night. Some have even heard the entity giggle down the hallway. The laughter of small children is also heard, especially in the courtyard or in the stairwells between floors. The children are seen in Victorian-era clothing and are usually kept in line by what people think is their grandmother. The story behind these three ghosts is that the children died after a bout with scarlet fever, and the grandmother looking after them felt guilty that she couldn't do more to help. Some reports state that it may be Elizabeth Poe watching over her grandchildren. The main bedroom is also a place with extra liveliness, including strange lights, shadows and numerous colorful orbs.

Linden Row Inn.

Another story concerns a girls' school that operated in the Row. A teenage girl fell out of a fourth-floor window and died. Her ghost is known to haunt the fourth floor. Sadly, I could find no other information about this girl in my research.

For another haunting experience, head to the Poe Museum at 1914 East Main Street (https://poemuseum.org). Opened in 1922, it has acquired the largest public collection of Poe artifacts and paraphernalia. There are also two black cats—Edgar and Pluto (from Poe's story "The Black Cat")—living in the back garden. Poe loved cats, and his favorite one, Catterina, sat on his shoulder while he wrote. Watch the upstairs of the museum and house, as two blond ghostly children have been seen in the windows.

Top: Poe Museum. *Bottom*: Poe's Pub.

For a great meal, head to Poe's Pub at 2706 East Main Street (https://www.poespubrva.com). Its menu is filled with Poe-inspired food, such as the Sloppy Poe and Raven Fries. There is also a Poe's Club sandwich and Poe's Famous Meatloaf. The food is delicious and comes with huge portions; nobody goes away hungry. Be sure to visit during their Unhappy Hour.

Linden Row Inn
100 East Franklin Street
Richmond, VA 23219
804-783-7000
https://www.lindenrowinn.com

DUNNLORA INN

Dunnlora Inn is a quaint and charming establishment that tries to keep some of the location's history alive while still providing a casual setting for its guests. Built in 1916 by George and Selina (pronounced "Se-lie-na") Erginbright, the inn functioned as both a family home and a boardinghouse for many years.

George hailed from Rockingham County, and Selina was a Gibson from Albemarle. George's father fought in the Civil War cavalry and had four horses shot out from under him, but he was never injured.

Mineral used to be a big mining town called Tolersville. Gold, pyrite, sulfur and vermiculite were found in the ground all over the town. Since so many mining families were coming to Mineral, the town decided to build 1,500 houses in the area to give these families a place to live. Unfortunately, the houses were never built, and people went bankrupt. George and Selina were dragged into this situation as well.

George supported his wife and two children (George Jr. and Ellis Anne) by working at a sawmill and living in company housing. George decided to partner with a Mr. Kennon, whose name graces the road running by the inn. Together, they bought a hotel, naming it the Mineral Hotel. They also owned a three-story hardware store, but it does not exist anymore.

No one knows if George Jr. ever lived in the finished house, but it is known that he helped in its construction. He was only a teenager when he was

Dunnlora Inn.

killed in 1916 following the explosion of tanks at the hardware store. He was rushed to Richmond Memorial Hospital, where he died ten hours later.

Shenia, one of the owners, says that George Jr. comes through often. During a public ghost investigation, while three teenage girls were sitting on a couch, someone noticed a stick figure on their structured light sensor (SLS) camera after Shenia had asked if George Jr. was present. The stick figure was lying across the laps of the girls, who said they felt ice cold at the time.

Tony and Shenia Wong purchased the house in 2016 with dreams of remodeling it into a bed-and-breakfast. All rooms are decorated with a specific period in mind. One space is an intimate sitting room, where guests can relax and enjoy the evening breezes. When guests wake up in the morning, a full breakfast is waiting downstairs. If guests aren't up for conversing, Shenia will have breakfast delivered to their room.

Several permanent residents haunt the inn, leading to unexplained occurrences for staff, visitors and guests. Among the events are objects moving from one place to another, shadows moving through the house, the sound of footsteps upstairs and of disembodied voices and even the ghost of a cat. The location is so active that ghost hunters far and wide have come to see what they can experience. On that list are Scott Porter from the Travel Channel's *Haunted Towns* and *Haunted Live*, Stephanie Burke from TLC's *Kindred Spirits* and Tonna and Lyle Lott from the Twisted Paranormal Society and the PBS show *The Twisted Realm*. Shenia states that despite all of these occurrences, only good spirits are at the inn. Bad ones are not allowed.

Tony and Shenia's renovation effort took two years, as they wanted to have everything perfect for future guests. All the changes stirred up ghostly activity in the house. Workers would find their equipment unplugged and doors slammed in their faces, and they would hear whistling or footsteps upstairs, but no one was ever found. Shenia says that since the renovations have been completed, there is activity, but not as much.

The most recent human death in the house was that of Mr. William Bennett, who passed away of natural causes in 1999 in one of the upstairs rooms. In fact, eight people have died in the house, all of natural causes. The cats showed up later and took over the house. Shenia told me that before they even got started, they had to remove all the litter boxes and food left over from when more than twenty cats lived in the house. Not surprisingly, there is a ghost cat that sometimes can be heard or felt by guests and during ghost hunts. Tony heard a cat meow and then felt it jump on the bed where he was sitting and walk around on top of the comforter. During one investigation, one of the team members brought a ball, and visible on an investigator's SLS camera was a ghost cat trying to get it away from them.

At first, Shenia was scared to be in the house alone because of all the activity. One day, she got up the courage to mop both the upstairs and downstairs floors. Plaster dust was all over from replacing and knocking down walls. She took her bucket of dirty water downstairs to empty and refill with clean water. When she returned upstairs, there were bare footprints in the dust on the floor, but only of a right foot, as if a person was hopping across the floor.

Shenia and her husband keep the inn closed securely at night, so no animals or people can enter. She went up to one of the bedrooms one morning and found a cat's paw prints and prints of an old woman's boot with a pointed toe and little heel.

A gentleman had come that Thursday to place a new security system for the inn, and Shenia wanted alarms on all the doors and cameras in specific places. On Sunday, Shenia was sweeping the dining room when the alarms started going off: "Front door open, evacuate!" The alarm system kept repeating the phrase. Shenia called Tony to come and shut it off, but when he tried to reset it, nothing happened. They finally got it to stop by pushing several buttons. They had no idea how they did it.

Tony went back outside. Not ten minutes later, the alarms started again. Shenia called him back to figure out what the problem was. Five minutes later, the alarms began again. Shenia figured that by this time, it was the spirits causing mischief. She stood at the bottom of the stairs and yelled, "If you don't stop the noise, I will come up there and sage you out of here." The alarms stopped on their own.

Fifteen minutes later, they went off again. Shenia and Tony called the guy from the security company to resolve the issue. When he arrived, he was bewildered. He explained that the alarms shouldn't be going off, as they had not yet been activated. He also stated the alarm wouldn't keep going off and that it would say "Front door open" or "Kitchen window open." It would not say, "Evacuate!" In fact, the word *evacuate* did not appear in any of the phrases used for the alarms.

They had another investigation lined up with Jessica Potter, a psychic medium, and once Shenia checked that everyone was ready for the event, she started to smell something like cannabis burning. She eventually realized it was sage and asked Jessica who was burning it. Jessica said that her friend David always burns sage before any event he does. Shenia told her he couldn't do that at the inn. For two different investigations, they got no activity at all.

After the last event, one of the spirits let Shenia know that David had run them away by burning the sage. She tried to explain that he wasn't trying to scare them, but then she remembered her threat about burning the sage if they didn't behave. The spirits left, but Shenia said they could come back, everything was fine now.

The funny thing about the cameras now is that when Shenia watches them, she can always hear people talking, but there is no one at the inn during these times. One day, she heard someone talking as loud as a normal person would speak. She also heard the front door open and the furniture being moved around. While chatting in the Blue Room upstairs, I heard thumping and other noises downstairs as well. One couple who stayed had been talking to Shenia on the side porch when they all heard knocking coming from inside the parlor. No one else was in the house at the time, so Shenia walked around the house. She found no one at the front door or in the parlor. The guest said, "But someone was knocking." Shenia simply replied, "Welcome to Dunnlora."

Shenia's daughter, Lacey, talked her into doing a ghost hunt at the inn. They are both sensitive and always see things, but Shenia didn't want to do it alone, so they invited two other ladies to join them. They got a little K2 and REM pod activity (these devices track spikes in electromagnetic energy and have multicolored lights noting motions near their sensors), but the two ladies decided to leave around 9:00 p.m. Lacey wanted to stay and see if anything might happen. They chose the Yellow Room and took their ovilus with them to see if they could communicate with the spirits. The ovilus uses single words and short phrases to allow for answers to any questions posed.

Shenia asked if anyone was with them, and the ovilus immediately said, "George." Shenia didn't know if it was George Sr. or Jr., though. The REM pod started lighting up as well. It has to be touched for it to respond. After the device started, all the other equipment started sounding alarms, too. This went on for about two minutes with no one near any of the equipment. When Shenia finally asked the spirit to back away from the REM pod, it went quiet. She asked the spirit to come back, and the REM pod started alarming again. She asked for them to step away again, and all noise stopped.

After all these occurrences, Shenia and Tony still wanted to open the inn as a bed-and-breakfast. In 2018, they opened for business while also taking reservations for weddings and graduations.

The Keurig coffee pot in the dining area has a unique history. Shenia's dad, who died in 2019, always loved some coffee just as he was getting ready to leave. That Christmas, she celebrated with her sisters, then came back to clean the inn after a holiday party. She and Tony wanted to leave around 7:30 p.m. to visit an old friend. They only drink coffee in the morning, so she thought it odd to hear the Keurig starting. She asked Tony why he was fixing coffee when they were trying to leave. He said that he never touched the machine. (The Keurig machine will indicate "Not ready" when it first starts; then it switches to "Ready to brew.") As Shenia walked past, the machine read "Not ready," so it had just started. She swears she never touched it. A week later, some friends were over for an investigation, and when one of them went to the kitchen, he watched the machine turn on by itself. He couldn't explain how it happened.

Another time, John and Lynn Harris from RVA Paranormal were doing an investigation, and they decided to have Mexican food for dinner. John had brought his own coffee and said he would have some when they returned. After eating, Shenia went home, and John and Lynn headed back to the inn. When they walked in the front door, Lynn called out, "Hello!" They both heard a woman answer, "Hello!," from upstairs. When they checked, the Keurig had already started, and no one was found in the house.

After breakfast the next morning, all three had a question-and-answer session with the spirits at the inn. Selina was the lady of the house, and Shenia gets her most of the time. They set up a REM pod, and Shenia started asking questions:

Q: Do I know you?
A: Long beep
Q: Is this someone I know?
A: Short beep
Q: Are you one of the spirits with the house?
A: Long beep
Q: Are you Selina?
A: Long beep
Q: Selina, are you glad we are keeping Dunnlora?
A: No answer
Q: Do you want us to sell Dunnlora?
A: No answer
Q: Are there any family members with me?
A: No answer

After Shenia and Tony opened the inn, they held a karaoke night in the parlor. A friend who joined them brought her four-year-old daughter,

Tabitha. Tabitha disappeared up the stairs for a bit. When she came back down, she had two handfuls of pennies. Shenia asked where she had found the pennies. Tabitha said she got them upstairs. Shenia queried the other adults, but no one had given her the pennies. Shenia questioned her again about where she found the pennies. Tabitha told her the little boy upstairs gave them to her. They walked upstairs so that Tabitha could show Shenia where the little boy was. Tabitha stood in the doorway of Selina's room and told Shenia that he was right there, then she pointed upward. Shenia asked if he was on the light fixture in the ceiling, and Tabitha replied that he was. He had come down, gave her the pennies, then crawled back up the wall like a lizard. Tabitha also said that he was sitting on the bench before and wanted her to come and play with him. Shenia figured the little boy was the orphan they had met before and must have liked playing with lizards, hence his manifestation.

One of the workers who was painting the outside of the house related a story to Shenia. He was working on the outside of a bathroom window, and the door to the bathroom that led into the bedroom was open. The painter started hearing what sounded like a man whistling in the bedroom, but he knew no one was in the house. When he looked up, he spotted a man come out of the bedroom and walk past the bathroom window. He said the man was older and wearing a white shirt. The man looked at the painter as if wondering what he was doing.

Before the bathroom event occurred, a ghost hunt was held, and the investigators wanted to check out the back stairs, where the butler's room is located. Shenia got a message from the spirit that his name was Kenny and that he was the gentleman everyone was seeing around the house. He was around sixty years old, possibly mentally challenged, and she felt that he was a member of the family but that they made him sit in the stairwell when they had parties at the house, as he wasn't allowed to attend. When Shenia stated this, the REM pod started alarming.

In fact, they have a recording in which they placed the REM pod on the stairs when they were doing a public investigation, and Shenia asked Kenny to come and touch the REM pod. She told him it was OK, that it was now her house and he had her permission. The REM pod began to light up, but the strange part on the recording is footsteps heard coming down the stairs and then the REM pod alarming.

Don Molnar (Haunted M.D.), who makes an appearance in the history of the Martha Washington Inn in this book, visited the Dunnlora after hearing about the activity. He brought his SLS camera. Shenia had been talking about Kenny at the time, so Don asked if Kenny was present in the room. On the SLS, they saw two stick figures at the top of the stairs, and Don asked if one of them was Kenny, could he wave? One of the figures immediately waved to them.

Don also told me that he caught some more SLS figures in the living room and saw a door unlatch by itself. The investigative group he was with recorded footsteps both on the back stairs and in the main entrance hallway.

There was also an instance in which a ghost man helped Tony and some friends finish patching their roof. Holes had accumulated in the roof where tin nails had worn down over the preceding one hundred years. Tony and his friends really didn't want to take the shingles down, as they had a raised type of print on them that looked like a fleur-de-lis. The men thought that it might be part of the family crest of George and Selina.

The two friends went up on the roof while Tony stayed in the attic. Tony knocked on the roof to direct them to the holes so they could caulk them under the shingles. They took a water hose with them to test the roof and make sure it didn't continue to leak. While this was transpiring, Shenia was in the Yellow Room throwing trash out the window while trying to clean the room. She thought at one point she had thrown her keys out with the trash. She called Tony down to help her find them, as she needed to leave shortly to go to an appointment. They finally discovered she had not thrown her keys out—they were in her coat pocket. She and Tony stood out front talking for about thirty minutes before she had to leave, and their contractor, Adam, looked down at Tony from the roof and asked how he had gotten down to the ground so fast. Tony told him that he had been down there for about thirty minutes already. Adam said there was no way that was true, because he had just heard Tony in the attic knocking and saying, "Here, Here!" Everyone was quite bewildered.

Friends of Tony's came out to see the new place and had their three-year-old son with them. The toddler was fast asleep as his father carried him while Shenia showed them around the inn. When they were getting ready to leave, the father placed his son in the car while his wife finished her conversation with Shenia. They began to drive off, then backed up the car once they got to the stop sign. The husband got out and spoke to Tony for a minute, and then they left again.

Tony called Shenia and explained what the father had told him. The little boy had still been asleep when they placed him in the car, but when they were ready to leave, he was awake. The father said his son kept pointing to the dining room window and saying, "creepy man."

George and Selina Erginbright.

When I visited, Shenia took me on a tour of the house and its surroundings. We started in the dining area, where the haunted coffee machine sits, and then we headed to the parlor across the hall. There is a side door that leads to a lovely porch, where chairs and tables are available for guests who may want to sit outside and enjoy the weather.

In the early 1900s, people visited the house on Sundays for tea and crumpets. As most people rode in carriages, there was a stable and a carriage house in the backyard. Make sure to take a full glance around the backyard. Shenia has a gorgeous pet duck named Chica that will walk around her house sometimes.

Moving back into the parlor, I was immediately pulled to the space in front of the fireplace and recliner. Something was definitely lurking near them, and Shenia replied that this particular room is very active. Selina is said to show up in pictures taken of the mirror above the fireplace. Shenia has been told by two different psychics that a tall woman in a Victorian dress with a cameo brooch and wearing her hair in a bun is always with her. Shenia is positive it is Selina they are describing. She says that Selina helped her decorate the inn by giving her a vision of what it should look like when she was finished. As Shenia told me, "An interior decorator—I am not!"

Shenia and her daughter, Lacey, decided to have a ghost hunt at the inn to help with finances. Shenia and Tony had purchased the house and sunk a lot of money into fixing and renovating both its interior and exterior. They decided to turn it into a bed-and-breakfast to recoup some of the money. Shenia didn't care what it looked like, but she had a vision of a warm, loving, grandmotherly house where the family could spend the holidays together.

On the second weekend, Shenia was sitting on the parlor floor and heard a woman say, "Mary Elizabeth," three times along with, "1942–43." She continued, "Mary is my name, Elizabeth is my child." Shenia found out that this person, while living, had stayed with relatives from another county because her mother wanted to keep her boyfriend away before she embarrassed the family and got pregnant. Unfortunately, she was already pregnant when she arrived at Dunnlora. She had the baby there, but no one knew what happened to the child after its birth. Some psychics told Shenia the baby died and was buried in the woods behind the house.

A couple of weeks later, Shenia told her friend Pam about the incident. Pam said she would speak to another friend, Shirley, who had grown up in Mineral, as did Shirley's parents. Shenia couldn't believe what Pam told her after the call to Shirley. Shirley's mother had been in school in Mineral, and there was a young girl who came from another town because her mother wanted to keep her away from her boyfriend. The inn had been a boardinghouse back then. She remembered the girl taking blood from dead chickens and placing it in her underclothes to hide her pregnancy.

A few months after that, while Shenia was cleaning the inn, a lady knocked on the door asking if the piano still sat in the parlor. The woman had lived in the house as a ten-year-old in 1954. Shenia told her the piano was gone, leaving the lady disappointed. She said she came to live with her grandparents, who were from northern Virginia, but her grandfather found the inn, and they stayed for six months.

After six months, they moved to Glen Allen, where the lady still lives today. Her husband passed away a few months before, and she woke up one morning determined to find Dunnlora again. She told Shenia that the lady who had run the boardinghouse, Sue Dunn, didn't seem to like kids very much. The visitor explained how she was plucking away one day on the piano, making Miss Sue ask if she knew how to play at all. The lady replied that she didn't, so Miss Sue told her to quit trying in the future. After the lady and Shenia talked for a bit, she left. Shenia called Pam and told her what the lady had said about living in the house. Pam surmised that the lady could have been the baby they had wondered about previously. Unfortunately, Shenia never got the lady's name, but she thought it was such a weird coincidence for them to research that information and then have this lady arrive out of the blue.

The side room off the parlor is a cozy and peaceful space with a massage table set up in the middle. Lacey performs Reiki and is also an aesthetician, one who gives facials and advanced skin care. The area used to be a wraparound porch with very little space, so they renovated the bathroom and placed some walls around the porch.

Heading upstairs, one sees many Civil War pictures and three gorgeous pictures of Shenia's daughters in their wedding gowns adorn the walls. The first room at the top of the stairs is the Sleeping Porch, which is a smaller room, but it is still gorgeously decorated. The next room is the Cottage Room. Its furniture is actually called cottage furniture, and Lacey found it in Madison County. Off the room is a sitting area that used to be a balcony porch, which still has the original flooring.

A little girl's spirit has been heard in here. Shenia did an investigation with several other people one evening and felt there was a little girl present. They had an ovilus, so someone asked, "How old are you?" The response came back, "ten."

They also discovered a little boy outside the doorway who was afraid to enter the bedroom. Both of the children were orphans, but they weren't siblings. Shenia researched to see if there had been an orphanage nearby, as the spirit children showed Shenia that when they often visited the back door, they received biscuits and pieces of apple pie.

Selina's Room is next, and it has some interesting stories. The bed came from an antiques dealer. There are rope burns on both sides of it. After the bed was placed in the room, every time Shenia got near it, she got sick. She even left and went home but still felt ill. She and Lacey set up a REM pod and a K2 on the bed. The day before, Shenia thought she sensed a man tied to the bed who may have had dementia. He thought his family was being mean to him by treating him this way. Shenia thought his name was Richard, so she asked him if that was correct, and the K2 went off immediately. This was a unique occurrence, due to the spirit being attached to the bed and not the location.

One day after they spoke to him again, Lacey told Richard that he didn't have to stay with the bed. He could leave if he wanted. Shenia also told him he was welcome to stay if he wanted. They got nothing else from him after that session.

Another couple stayed in Selina's Room, and both persons had an unusual experience, which they didn't tell the other about until the next morning at breakfast. They came down for breakfast, and Shenia asked how their night had been. The lady said she had been lying in bed with the lights off and felt something brushing against her face, which she thought was a moth. She just brushed it away and went back to sleep.

Her husband chimed in and told his wife what had happened to him. He had gone to the bathroom in the middle of the night. As he came back to the bedroom, he looked over at his wife and saw a little girl rubbing her face. The little girl then sank into the floor and disappeared.

The Williamsburg Room has had its share of happenings as well. A Greek lady stayed in the room one night and awoke to find a little boy, about four years old, standing at the foot of the bed. He had on bib overalls and climbed up on the bed and crawled toward her. The woman started screaming and told him, "Go away!" He disappeared when her husband woke up and asked what was wrong. She started feeling nauseous and didn't eat much breakfast. The woman and her husband told Shenia that after they left and got some distance between them and the inn, she started to feel much better.

Shenia and her husband, Tony, usually stay in this room if they spend the night. One evening, they were watching TV when they heard what sounded like a man pacing in front of their door. She asked Tony if he heard it. He said that he did. When she asked if he was going to check it out, he said that he wasn't.

During one investigation, a girl was sitting on the floor and started yelling that there was a cat in the room. She said she saw it go under the bed. The inn does have a ghost cat on the premises; however, Shenia has no pets. Shenia's grandson has even chased it under the bed, yelling, "Here, kitty kitty!"

George and Selina deeded the house to their nieces, Marion and Sue Dunn, as George was going bankrupt. Sue Dunn ran the boardinghouse with Marion's help. Sue had adopted her niece Sara Ward, who was a sickly child. Her sister had other children and couldn't take care of Sara properly. Shenia and Lacey were in the Williamsburg Room when two visitors asked if there were hard feelings about the baby going to her sister. The door to the room slowly moved and closed. There was no wind coming from the window.

To further prove that it wasn't the wind that made the door move back and forth, Adam took a bucket of plaster, roughly twenty pounds, and placed it in front of the door. When the question was asked again about hard feelings, one could visibly see the door trying to close, which it did halfway. No one was near the bucket at the time.

Scott Porter and Stephanie Burke joined an investigation at the inn one weekend. Scott had told everyone that he had been studying his genealogy. Stephanie, who is a psychic medium, told Shenia that there were not only many spirits in the house but also that some were attached to the land around the property. During the investigation, Stephanie wanted to play Native American chanting and music as well as Civil War songs. The group split up and set up their equipment in different parts of the house. Some of the guests recorded musket fire outside the house, which they thought could have been from skirmishes in the Battle of Trevilian Station. A cannonball had been found by a previous owner in the garden area.

Scott and Stephanie led the investigation, but everyone chose where they wanted to be on the stairs to observe. Shenia was standing in the middle of the stairs; others were at both the top and the bottom. Once everyone was settled, Stephanie played the Native American chanting, which was weird to Shenia, because Lacey had heard chanting near the same spot on the stairs the week before.

As the recording was played, they saw a shadow figure come out of the floor near the bottom of the stairs. Once it started up the stairs, all the equipment began to alarm, indicating something nearby. At about the middle of the stairs, the figure changed into a Native American. Shenia could see a type of headdress. Scott stated that when it came toward him, it felt like electricity. Another person, who had never participated in a ghost hunt, started screaming. This caused the figure to walk through the wall and come out the other side. On the other side of the wall is a picture of a Native American. Stephanie told Scott the figure was a Native American medicine man and was coming to say "brother" to Scott.

Years before this, Angel, a friend of Shenia's who is also a psychic medium, asked her about earthquakes in the area. There had been an earthquake in Virginia the previous year in that region. Angel told her it had awakened this medicine man, who was protective of the land.

Scott returned to Tennessee and worked on his genealogy some more. His grandfather was in his nineties at the time, so Scott asked him about a lady Scott found in his research named Betsy. Betsy and her sister had married brothers, but that was all the information Scott could find on them. He asked if his grandfather knew any more about the lady and her sister.

Scott's grandfather said he wouldn't find anything else, because both women were Native Americans, and back then, that wasn't a good thing. Scott kept looking for Betsy and discovered that she was the wife of Hanging Maw, chief of the Overhill Cherokees from 1788 to 1794. It seemed that Scott may have had royal blood. That is why the investigators think the medicine man went to Scott that night. Shenia said that the spirits sometimes know a lot more than we do.

A good example of this is how spirits will listen and learn things from us in the present. Selina told Shenia that she was upset with both Tony and Rusty for cutting down her pink azalea bush. The bush had come halfway up the window when they bought the property. Shenia had gone out one day, and when she came back, the bush was gone. Shenia asked Tony about the bush. He told her Rusty cut it down. The bush was gone, and they couldn't do anything about it.

A year later, Selina asked about it again. She was still upset, as an aunt had given her the azalea bush as a housewarming gift. She specifically told Shenia that Tony told Rusty to cut it down. Rusty argued that Shenia would be upset, and Tony said not to worry about it. Shenia went to Tony again and asked if he told Rusty to cut it down. Tony replied that he hadn't. About this time, they both heard loud male footsteps on the stairs and the sound of a measuring tape opening and closing. Tony just happened to have one in his hand, but he hadn't used it while he was talking to Shenia.

A few days later, Rusty was cleaning one of the bathrooms. Shenia asked if Tony had told him to cut the bush down. He said no, but Shenia kept insisting that Tony had told him to do it. Rusty finally asked why she kept saying that. She told him Selina told her the gist of the conversation and what had happened. Rusty finally admitted that Tony told him to cut the bush down.

Dunnlora Inn
903 Mineral Avenue
Mineral, VA 23117
540-259-9173
https://www.dunnlorainn.com

4

FREDERICKSBURG, ALEXANDRIA & MANASSAS

BELLE GROVE PLANTATION

Established in 1670 and located on the Port Conway riverfront, this historic plantation's claim to fame is being the birthplace of James Madison, fourth president of the United States, in 1751. It served as a one-thousand-acre tobacco plantation as well as a headquarters for the Union army during the Civil War. Each of the four rooms is named after a family that owned the property: Madison, Turner, Conway and Hipkins-Bernard.

The first family to purchase the property was the Conways. They lived in the home for around 120 years. Nellie Conway (Eleanor Rose) met James Madison Sr. after he came to ship tobacco out to other ports. She returned to Belle Grove pregnant with James Madison Jr. However, with smallpox raging through Orange County, James Jr. stayed at Belle Grove until he was two years old, then joined his mom in Orange County.

The property was subsequently sold to the Hipkins-Bernard family. The beautiful manor, built in 1790–92 for Fanny Hipkins, incorporated the original structure of the present house. Fanny lived there until she died in 1801 and is buried on the property.

In 1839, Carolinus Turner took over the estate and organized a proper home for a wife, as he planned to marry in the future. After ten years, he married Susan Augusta Rose. She was seventeen; he was forty-two. It was common in those days for a man to be much older than his wife. They had five beautiful children and lived through the Civil War.

Belle Grove Plantation. Is that a lady ghost with a white dress in the right window beside the door?

The Union army occupied the manor in 1861, using it as a headquarters. When they left, they took all the family's livestock, although they did allow the Turners' nine-year-old son, George, to keep his pony. When the family finally returned after the army departed, they lived in the house until 1894.

The Taylor-Thornton family purchased the property in 1894, but the deed didn't stay with them long and passed through several other families until 1930. The Hooker family lived there until 1981, with their son staying until 1987. With so many families owning the estate, the house fell into further disrepair with each exchange. Mrs. Hooker's son allowed the house to deteriorate, letting the roof collapse and the floors rot.

Finally, in 1987, the Haas family took over the deed. They did major renovations, which took six years and cost $3.5 million. The house was restored to its former glory. Unfortunately, the Hookers' son sold all the chandeliers, so no originals remain. For the most part, everything else in the house is original, except for the plaster, updated plumbing and modern appliances.

Michelle and Brett Darnell currently run the lavish bed-and-breakfast. Michelle knew it was haunted the first time they went to see the property. They took a tour of the whole plantation, and Michelle decided to take some pictures. The property manager walked with her until she arrived at the basement door. He decided to wait outside with her family while Michelle finished her photography. Walking over to the second room from the door to get a good shot, Michelle heard the basement door slam. She thought the property manager had changed his mind and decided to join her, but she didn't see him come down, so she headed back upstairs. The basement door was now closed. When she opened it, she could see her family and the manager standing outside the window. She was the only one in the house at the time.

The first entity Michelle met was a six-foot-tall field-working enslaved man named Nathaniel. She heard him speak to her while she was in the basement placing laundry in the dryer. He came up behind her and muttered something in her ear, which scared her enough to make her run back upstairs. She later told him that he can't do that anymore, because it scares her. He has behaved ever since. Michelle now leaves Nathaniel in charge of the home whenever she goes out for the day.

Many other happenings have taken place within the walls of Belle Grove, which is thought to be one of the most haunted locations in Virginia. The Lady in White was first seen in 2012 wandering the Turner Suite in the middle of the day and the Madison Suite late at night. She often appears to the men in the rooms rather than the women. Watch for her on the carriage side of the upper balcony. Visitors and guests sometimes see a lady in a white gown with long black hair.

Michelle had a paranormal investigation team filming and recording one night. Around 1:00 a.m., everyone went outside to take a break. Looking back at the house, one investigator noted that it had a really creepy appearance. Michelle insisted it looked absolutely beautiful with all the stars and the moon behind it. She happened to glance at the balcony near the Madison Room. Before she could tell anyone what she saw, another crew member said they saw the Lady in White. They retrieved a flashlight to find her, but she quickly disappeared. A pregnant lady decided to take a nap after an exhausting afternoon, and she woke to the Lady in White sitting in a chair watching her. There is speculation that the lady is a daughter of Mr. Turner, maybe Carrie, but this can't be confirmed.

A young boy named Jacob was discovered in 2013. He likes to move items around, turn electrical devices on and play with balls. He has been photographed looking out a window. Michelle and Brett believe he is five years old, as there is a recording of him saying this. A family cemetery on the property has two kids buried in it. Could one of them be Jacob?

Jacob can be quite mischievous. Michelle was making tea one morning and needed a spoon to stir the ingredients. She placed it on the counter, went to retrieve some items and found it missing when she returned. She told Jacob to put the spoon back when he was finished with it. An hour later, the spoon appeared on the counter. He is also known for moving Michelle's knives from one drawer to another. Jacob also made an LED ring sitting in the center of a table bounce all the way to the edge and fall on the floor. No one was near the area at the time.

The other little girl, Rose, who is thought to be between six and eight years old, loves to play with people's hair. Michelle was sitting at the table in the dining room working on her computer when she felt fingers going from her neck up to the top of her head. She quickly pulled away, asking the spirit not to play with her hair.

Two ghostly cats hang out all over the house. Their favorite location is the Conway Suite, where they were first heard in 2013. A picture was taken in 2014 of an upstairs window with both cats. Some guests and staff have heard a cat meow in the room. They are also known to purr in guests' ears, meow loudly and walk across beds while guests are trying to sleep. The Center for Paranormal Research and Investigation (CPRI) visited the property to do its own research. Its members caught an EVP of a cat meowing in the background when none were present in the surrounding area. The plantation has no cats on the property—or does it?

Guests continually ask Michelle where her cats went so quickly. The cats are a yellow tabby and a dark gray. One guest went to thank Michelle for her hospitality during her stay and saw a yellow tabby sitting by Michelle's door. Michelle explained that she didn't have a cat, but both the guest and her husband saw the animal.

At a wedding, an eleven-year-old boy and his grandmother asked Michelle the names of her two cats, both of which had been seen in their rooms. Michelle explained once again that she had no cats on the premises.

Union soldiers are still hanging out and fighting the war. Guests have seen and heard them marching past their window and into the fields, standing guard to protect against invading enemies. Four soldiers in the garage turn electrical devices on at different intervals. When Michelle was leaving one late afternoon, she turned to go to her car and told the spirits that it was getting dark and asked if they could at least turn the light on for her. Now whenever she gets near the end of the circle driveway, nearly one hundred yards away, the light turns on for her. She says the soldiers take their jobs very seriously.

Another spirit the staff has heard is that of Mary Hooker, who lived at Belle Grove from 1930 to 1981. When a room is being cleaned after the departure of a guest, Mary appears to make sure it is done correctly. The staff have a good idea that the spirit is Mary Hooker, as she was caught saying her name in an EVP session.

The majestic inn has been featured on several paranormal shows. *Kindred Spirits with Amy & Adam* spent some time in the caretaker's house. The entity in this location (Baldwin Lee) is belligerent and abusive, especially to Michelle. As soon as Michelle stepped through the front door, she became depressed and upset, as her sensitivity to spirits allowed her to be affected by Baldwin's strong emotions. Michelle left and refused to return. The investigators discovered that the angry spirit just wants people to stay out of his house. They believe the caretaker's house once belonged to Lee and that he controls what happens within its walls and doesn't like anyone to enter it. Baldwin Lee, buried in a small cemetery near the plantation, fits this description perfectly. His ghost shouted obscenities at anyone who dared to speak to him. Amy tried speaking to him with quiet tones, and Baldwin responded in kind.

The reason Amy and Adam spent the night in the caretaker's house was to film and record any activity. In the morning, Amy came downstairs and spread out all her notes on the dining room table. While she studied them, loud banging began on the dining room wall. She recorded the noise with her phone to show Adam. They never could figure out what was causing the noise.

Adam found out that the Lady in White sometimes appeared in the room where he was staying. He hoped to catch a glimpse of her while there, but she never appeared. While watching video of the rooms they recorded, he noticed dancing lights on the walls, but the source was never found. Disembodied voices were also common to hear at this location.

After this particular episode, Amy and Adam decided to try one more time to clear the air between Michelle and Baldwin. Michelle even went to his burial site to find a neutral ground where they could talk. She discovered that Baldwin was holding other spirits with him, possibly other enslaved persons, because he did not want to be alone. Michelle promised that if he let the other entities leave, he would never be alone and that she would come to visit him often. After speaking to him at the cemetery, she told him it was time to return to Belle Grove. When Michelle walked into his house, Baldwin made a loud banging noise. Michelle said the house didn't feel as depressed or negative as it had before their talk. She realizes that he feels safe in his house, and she wants to help him feel settled. She told him he could stay as long as he wanted, but he couldn't be mean, scare people or show up in pictures as a skeleton to those who visit him. Everyone should be able to exist together there. Using a flashlight for yes and no answers, she inquired if Baldwin understood what she was saying. The flashlight turned off promptly.

RVA Paranormal did an investigation in several rooms known to have activity. They headed to the basement and were excited to obtain an EVP. They asked the entity present how many people were in the room at the time. You can clearly hear the voice say, "seven." Both a REM pod and a spirit box (ovilus) helped discern if any entities wished to communicate. When asked if the spirit wanted to change colors on the REM pod, the answer was "nope." The spirit, asked to change the color again, answered, "OK." One of the most interesting answers came after asking the spirit to name someone it loved. The answer that came back was "Ana," who they later discovered was a former cook at the house.

The group also checked out the Turner Suite and asked the entity there if Mrs. Turner had died in that very room. The answer came back, "yes." In the parlor, a "meow" is heard coming from one of the ghost cats. Organ sounds were heard coming from the parlor, although there wasn't one present. When the investigators visited the Summer Kitchen, they heard, "Get out!" several times. The caretaker's house had a flurry of activity, including footsteps, doors slamming, knocking on walls and a dog barking.

Argos Paranormal also did an investigation and used a laser grid in one room to catch something walking by the equipment or breaking the light field. Starting in the Turner Room, when they asked if anyone was present, they heard a distinct, "hello." One spirit even asked, "Where am I?" The investigator asked the spirit if it was lost. The spirit answered back, "You can't help me." A few seconds later, "dead" was heard.

They headed to the library, where one of their lanterns kept turning on and off by itself. Beside the lantern, they had a parascope, which lights up different colors when any energy is near it. This time, it turned red and green. One of the flashlights even turned on when the investigators asked if John Hooker was present in the room. They asked him to light up the parascope, and it started flashing all the colors.

In the Madison Room, one investigator felt something poke him in the arm when they first arrived. They thought maybe it was Jacob playing and told the spirit to turn one of the flashlights on for them. The spirit replied, "I'm sorry, I shouldn't." They also asked about Mr. Hooker and if he was available to talk. "Come find me," then "kitchen room," were heard. Asking Jacob one more time if he wanted to talk to them, he said, "Come find the ball." They also started seeing a few orbs in the room climb up an investigator's leg and up a nearby curtain.

In the slave quarters, they did a spirit box session, asking if anyone was present with them. They heard, "help," then, "me." They talked for a while with no responses then asked if there was anything the spirit wanted to say to them. "Go away," was the answer. They told the spirit they would go and bade it goodnight. Over the voice recorder, you can hear someone respond, "goodnight."

The most interesting thing about the tour is the laser grid in the parlor near the end of the video (https://www.youtube.com/watch?v=G3F1guE80h4). A figure is seen breaking the lines and moving across the room. In the dining room, there is footage of a flashlight moving back and forth by itself.

There are so many paranormal entities at this location that guests may not get to meet or see them all. Guests and visitors should respect the spirits who live there, lest they follow the guests home and cause more mischief.

Belle Grove Plantation
9221 Belle Grove Drive
King George, VA 22485
540-621-7340
https://www.bellegroveplantation.com

RICHARD JOHNSTON INN & 1890 CAROLINE HOUSE

Built in 1770, this inn was designed by John Taylow, one of the many signers of the Declaration of Independence. After surviving both the Revolutionary and Civil Wars, the property has been transformed from two row houses into one larger lodge. There are different rooms to be seen when one is in the back courtyard. Room 9 housed the original kitchen, while Rooms 10 and 11 were employed as slave quarters.

Richard Johnston and his family lived here in the early 1800s while he served as mayor of Fredericksburg. Some of the furnishings are original, such as the flooring and fireplaces. One of the rooms upstairs even has a burnt beam near the wall from a fire that occurred during the Civil War. Large-caliber bullet holes can be found in the walls from the fighting that took place in the area.

The property exchanged hands several times through the years. It became a "cold water flat" in the 1930s, meaning it had no running water or central heating. After 1970, Hunter Greenlaw bought the inn, which was a warehouse at the time, and renovated the entire property. He used one side for his office and turned the back side into a fancy eatery with individual shops.

Richard Johnston Inn.

Finally, in 1993, Susan Thrush purchased the inn. She operated it until 2001, when Charles Leopold took over the deed. At this time, another renovation took place, replacing everything from the beds to the linens. Cable and internet access were added.

Several friendly ghosts linger at the Richard Johnston Inn. One is David, who acted as a sharpshooter for the Confederate army. He can be heard upstairs walking around in his boots. He is also known to sit at the kitchen counter when the owner is working or cutting up fruits and vegetables. I experienced cold chills on entering the kitchen and felt as though something pulled me in there. On my recording, I heard what sounded like a metal trash can lid banging, but no one else was in the room. Betsy, one of the two innkeepers, also said the kitchen door will swing back on her at times, even though it has a stopper on it. I never sensed any malevolence; these spirits seem very friendly and a little mischievous, depending on what story is told.

Toby is another entity that resides at the inn. He is believed to be about ten years old and lived as an enslaved person before the Civil War. He is a mischievous fellow who likes to rearrange silverware on the table when no

Staircase where Beth saw the elderly African American gentleman standing on the landing.

one is looking. Research also shows that he may have been hanged from one of the tall trees behind the inn after he was caught stealing bacon.

Beth, another innkeeper, related a story about a time she was showing guests to their room and happened to glance up the stairs opposite the front door and saw an older African American man standing there. She answered a guest's question and looked back; the man was no longer there. Asking her coworker if anyone was on that side of the house at the time, Betsy said that those rooms were empty.

Beth says that although there are some unseen guests, she isn't afraid to spend the night. She receives only good vibes from the entities.

Beth gave me a tour of the unoccupied rooms that day. Heading up to the Virginian Room on the second floor, the same steps were taken as when Beth had seen the older gentleman. Reaching the landing, I felt cold chills and a burst of energy.

There is a large cabinet in the room that doubles as closet space. A couple spent the night in this room, and the wife had a very uncomfortable time sleeping due to the cabinet doors shaking during the night, as if someone were trying to open them without turning the handle. Her husband slept through the racket.

I also asked about experiences Beth has had since working at the inn. She and Betsy both hear noises, footsteps and whistling, but they never find the source or anyone else in the inn. I noticed a gentle feeling in the Virginian Room.

The next room to visit was the Old Town Room. A magnificent hand-painted mural of historic Fredericksburg hangs on the wall above the head of the bed. There is a rafter on the left side of the room near the bed that shows signs of fire damage. Many guests request this room to meet the friendly ghosts who inhabit it. When she is cleaning, Betsy will mash the

Cabinet with doors that shake all night. Something was trying to open them without turning the handle.

toilet paper down so it won't roll off. On multiple occasions, she has left to get some cleaning supplies and come back to the toilet paper rolled to the floor from where it had been sitting on the shelf.

A retired dentist staying at the Caroline House, the other part of the inn, told Beth about the location being his grandmother's house when she was

Old Town Room with gorgeous mural behind the bed.

alive. He was in his seventies, but he remembered playing in the rooms over the garage, which have now been converted into a suite. He started to choke on something once while he was eating. He said that a force came from behind and pushed him hard into a table, and the food popped out onto the floor. Photographs have been taken of an apparition in that suite. Is Grandma still watching over her guests?

Richard Johnston Inn & 1890 Caroline House
711 Caroline Street
Fredericksburg, VA 22401
540-899-7606
https://www.therichardjohnstoninn.com

The Alexandrian

The former Hotel Monaco, located at the corner of King and Pitt Streets in Alexandria, is a unique lodging choice. I have stayed at this location many times throughout the years. Each time, the hotel staff was welcoming and made me feel right at home. It is a dog-friendly hotel that provides a bowl of cold water outside the entrance for thirsty canine companions.

However on December 20, 2016, Marriott took over management of the hotel, renaming it the Alexandrian. Even as the hotel changed hands, there was no denying the history of people dying there and shadows moving in the dark hallways.

The original property, known as the Marshall House, was standing at the start of the Civil War in 1861. Colonel Elmer E. Ellsworth, a close acquaintance and an assistant to President Abraham Lincoln, tried to retrieve a Confederate flag from the roof of the house. The owner, James W. Jackson, who raised a huge secession flag after Virginia decided to secede, shot and killed Ellsworth on May 24, 1861. These were said to be some of the first shots of the war. Jackson lost his life moments later, when Private Francis Brownell, assisting Ellsworth in stealing the flag, stabbed him several times with his bayonet. Ellsworth was the first Union officer to die while skirting the town. Brownell received a Medal of Honor for his bravery.

President Lincoln kept the Confederate flag. His son Tad used to play with it and wave it at parades. Pieces of the flag have been saved through the years and can be found at different historical museums, such as New York State Military Museum & Veterans Research Center, the Smithsonian Institution's National Museum of American History in Washington, D.C., and the Fort Ward Museum and Historic Site in Alexandria.

After the war, several small businesses moved into the Marshall House. A fire in 1873 brought about a great deal of reconstruction, and the house was finally torn down in 1950.

A plaque hung on the wall of the Hotel Monaco explaining that Jackson was the first martyr in the cause of "Southern Independence." In October 2017, Marriott had it removed and given to the United Daughters of the Confederacy.

The gunfight and stabbing occurred in the old staircase of the Marshall House. Currently, it is the sixth floor of the Alexandrian. The opposing sides are still fighting over the flag to this day. Some employees refuse to go up to the sixth floor, because they see things they can't explain. It is thought the altercation that killed both men is ongoing, and some employees may have witnessed the fight. Many guests have seen shadows lurking in the hallways, as well as a few other sightings on the sixth floor.

I photographed two of the stairwells on the southeast corner of the hotel but didn't see any entities in the pictures. But, checking the recording, I heard sounds that weren't there when I visited the area. In stairwell G, there was a sound like wind blowing down the staircase. In stairwell E, there was extraneous noise that sounded like old-fashioned music playing.

For another short side trip, head to the Carlyle House at 121 North Fairfax Street. The Mansion House Hotel used to sit in front of the home. It is gone

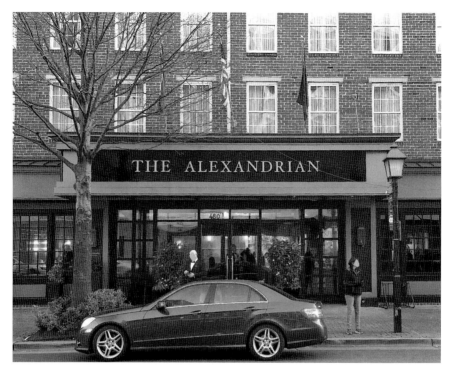

The Alexandrian (formerly Hotel Monaco).

The Carlyle House.

now, but in the past, it served as a Union hospital after Alexandria was seized during the Civil War. Patients would jump from the upper floors to stop their suffering. Apparently, on Fairfax Street, some ghostly patients are still jumping and falling in that same location.

Some paranormal investigators believe ghosts other than patients may still haunt the property. After the Carlyles lost their house and land, James Green purchased the site with plans to transform it into the Mansion House Hotel. Looking at the buildings beside the Carlyle House, indentations can still be seen where bricks were placed to help support a walkway between the two properties. While building the walkway, three construction workers fell to their deaths. Apparently, these men continue to haunt the property. As a side note, on my recording, I heard a "womp, womp" sound when entering the site. There was nothing around that could have contributed to it, and I was alone at the time.

The Carlyle House (www.novaparks.com/parks/carlyle-house-historic-park) has its own ghost: Syble. She was the second wife of John Carlyle. Extremely jealous of John's first wife, Sarah, Syble burned all of Sarah's possessions and refused to mention her name after moving into the house. Pictures taken both inside and outside the house have shown different-colored orbs. Some experts say that enlarging the photographs will bring out faces within the orbs.

The Alexandrian (formerly Hotel Monaco)
480 King Street
Alexandria, VA 22314
703-549-6080
https://thealexandrian.com

OLDE TOWNE INN

Located in Manassas, this historic inn incorporates a tavern and dining area on the first floor with guest rooms on the second. Many travelers and residents who were caught between two Civil War battles—The First Battle of Bull Run in 1861 and the Second Battle of Bull Run in 1862—stayed at the inn when they needed lodging or a hot meal. Apparently, many Union soldiers also took up residence here during the war.

Olde Towne Inn.

Miss Lucy is thought to have been an employee or daughter of the inn's initial owner. She may have had to pack up and leave her home during the war or possibly lost a loved one on the battlefield. She makes her presence known in different ways: making loud noises, turning on faucets, pulling people's feet and poking them when they are sleeping, moving objects to different spots and playing with electrical devices. She does not like to upset children and is very calm when around them. Most people can feel her presence and describe it as someone with interest, not malevolence. She is seen in Rooms 50, 52 and 54 and sometimes in the hotel tavern, which is now closed. The owners and staff seem to think she is from the Civil War era. The inn has a restaurant, and there is plenty of lodging for tourists traversing Washington and surrounding areas.

Two guests staying in Room 54 reported that something kept pulling on their mattress. The hotel staff told them it was Miss Lucy being mischievous. Another couple staying in Room 54 had strange experiences as well. The wife said she heard something crash to the bathroom floor, but when she checked to see what had happened, nothing was broken or had fallen. She and her husband decided to relax and go back to sleep. Miss Lucy struck again and started pulling on the edge of the mattress. The couple thought a wild animal had gotten loose, and they started searching the room to rid themselves of the critter. No animal was ever found. They tried one more time to go back to sleep, but the wife said she watched her husband floating above the bed. He then was "let go," fell back on the bed and rolled to the floor.

A guest who worked in construction stayed in one of the haunted rooms after a long day at work. As soon as he placed his suitcase on the bed, it felt as though someone had kicked the bedpost. He then checked to make sure he was alone in the room. Finding no one, he thought maybe a guest in the next room had hit the wall too hard by mistake. He was awakened in the night by someone or something moving around on his bed. He jumped up and turned all the lights on, causing the movement to stop.

Again, he searched the room. Finding no one, he turned the light off and lay back down. As soon as he got comfortable, footsteps were heard running across the carpet. Something then grabbed his feet, but he shook it off several times.

The hotel staff says that Miss Lucy stays in Room 52 but sometimes likes to wander to the tavern. A family was in the tavern eating breakfast when a woman in a nightgown and an old coat stopped to ask the wife where she could pick up a to-go order. The husband came back after paying the bill, and the wife explained what the lady had wanted. Her husband asked her, "What lady?" He had not seen anyone approach her. Maybe Miss Lucy was hungry after wandering the hotel. The tavern is closed at present.

A review was left for specific rooms from guests (a woman and her mother) who had previously stayed there. They asked specifically for the haunted rooms, but the staff placed them in Room 51. Rooms 52 and 54 are most active. The guests stated that the toilet kept flushing without stopping. After dinner, they came back to find the shower broken. The staff moved them to Room 52.

Stranger things started to happen once they switched. There was no dial tone on the phone, and a loud shuffling of feet across the carpet could be heard. The door opened by itself several times. According to Maggie Cecilia P., as of 2016, they were planning their next visit.

When I spoke to the manager, Shawna, about Miss Lucy, she had a couple of stories to tell. One guest wound up locked in his room for several hours because the key wouldn't open the door. The days of actual keys are

Haunted Rooms 51–54.

long gone, and this hotel employs electrical door locks that use key cards. Sometimes, they just do not work, especially for Rooms 51–54.

Shawna also told me about a gentleman guest, about twenty-four years old, who looked and acted normal when he checked in for the night. The clerk placed him in Room 47 or 49, near Room 51 and the hauntings. He ran down to the main lobby in the middle of the night, screaming that a ghost was chasing him around his room. He was visibly frightened and wanted the clerk to go see for herself. The clerk went up to his room and found nothing to validate his claim. The guest came back the second day and had to be escorted off the property by the police. The hotel refused to give him a refund based on the claim that a ghost had chased him around his room. One wonders if Miss Lucy was just having some fun and finding a new room to haunt.

Olde Towne Inn
9403 Main Street
Manassas, VA 20110
703-368-9191
https://theoldetowneinn.com/

WAYSIDE INN

Founded in 1797, Wayside Inn is one of the oldest taverns and dining locations in Virginia. It is also said to be one of the most haunted. It served as a refuge for both the Union and Confederacy during the Civil War, and soldiers in both blue and gray uniforms still appear to be hanging around, frequently visiting the lobby. Room 14 is considered to be the most active.

Back in 1797, after travelers crossed the Shenandoah Valley, they would stop at this inn, which was then known as Wilkenson's Tavern. The site also became a stopover for people to rest or to water their horses.

In the early 1900s, Samuel Rhodes purchased the property, adding wings on both sides and a third floor. He renamed it the Wayside Inn. After the roads were paved and cars started traveling through the valley, the inn was known as "America's First Motor Inn." When Leo Bernstein purchased the property in 1960, he tried to restore all of the rooms by giving them a unique look and feel. The current owners, George and Becky Reeves, are doing their best to preserve its historic heritage.

One of the innkeepers says that a cold spot is located near the fireplace. An employee was shocked to see a woman in a long dress appear in front of him there. Other workers say the woman is wearing a blue dress with a white collar. The cold spot seems to hover around her. This leaves the owners and employees to wonder if the fireplace is emanating these spirits.

There are plenty of other strange happenings at the location. These include the sounds of children running in the hallway when there are none nearby, the sounds of disembodied voices throughout the inn, objects and belongings being moved to other locations and guests who leave coins out during the night waking to find them fashioned into the letter *L*.

Both the old slave kitchen and the regular kitchen are teeming with activity. Something continually unties the dishwasher's apron and knocks dishes onto the floor in the regular kitchen. In the old slave kitchen, devices stop working after the batteries inexplicably die. One paranormal investigator took a picture that revealed an outline of a soldier through a window. On the other side of the wall where the investigator stood, there was a stable, and he recorded horse sounds in the location.

Employees say that in the slave quarters, which is the oldest part of the inn, footsteps can be heard coming up to the front door. When they investigate, no one is found near the door. The inn's history is rumored to include a stint as a Civil War hospital. Many soldiers never made it back home. Employees have seen shadows pass by the windows after dark. These were thought to be from headlights, but no vehicles were in front of the building or going down the road at the time.

Members of the night staff hear people talking all the time while they are working, but no one is ever found in the area. One worker said someone breathed on her neck while she walked through the older part of the inn. Some of the evening staff, while waiting for the night shift to arrive, heard footsteps at 11:15 p.m. every so often. Assuming it was the night shift, they waited to greet them, but no one ever came through the doorway. Some have reported the ghost of a young girl in Room 9. They also reported feeling a presence in Rooms 22 and 23.

Witnesses believe all the ghosts are friendly and benevolent, although Room 14 makes people uneasy and has more reported paranormal activity than any other area. Most of the housekeeping staff refuses to enter the room. One guest stated that she heard battlefield noises. Her daughter felt something in the bed with her. She awoke to an older soldier complaining that she was on his side of the bed. What else could she do but move to the other side?

Other guests took their dowsing rods and tried to communicate with the gentleman. They asked if he lived at the inn or was just passing through. He replied "no" to both queries. They tried their spirit box, and the gentleman told them, "I'm sick." They noted that as they spoke to the spirit, the canopy fringes on the bed waved back and forth. The room is thought to be haunted by a previous guest who apparently never left the establishment.

Wayside Inn
7783 Main Street
Middletown, VA 22645
540-869-1797
https://www.waysideinn1797.com

BLACK HORSE INN

When visiting this country inn, I entered through the front; on both sides of the entryway, staircases lead to the upper floor. These stairs are rumored to be tapped on by the Dancing Ghost. After meeting Michelle, a chef, who was hanging out in the kitchen, I immediately noticed the old wavy windows in the kitchen and remembered seeing them at Tuckahoe Plantation as well. (Wavy windows indicate that the structure is older, perhaps from the 1800s, and has history.)

The Black Horse Inn is believed to be haunted by four entities, and guests say they have seen strange activity. Voices and laughter are heard when rooms are empty, and objects seem to fall over or off shelves by themselves. One entity likes to leave impressions on the Burgundy Room bed. The Dancing Ghost likes to tap-dance on the stairs. Another ghost knocks over Christmas trees, causing ornaments and bulbs to break. The employees have nicknamed him Scrooge. The last entity is a laughing Civil War nurse.

Built in the 1850s, this historic inn borrowed its name from a Confederate unit in the First Battle of Bull Run. The Black Horse Cavalry beat the Union forces and received praise from Jefferson Davis, the Confederate president. History shows that the location once served as a Civil War hospital, which leads to some of the stories about the hauntings. Michelle confirmed that the front two rooms—a dining room and a sitting room—

Black Horse Inn. *Courtesy of Michael Schwartz.*

served as a makeshift hospital during the Civil War. Ownership of the inn went through sixty-five hands during the war, especially from the Confederate army to the Union army.

Dr. Sprague bought the inn in the 1920s and decided to renovate the entire property. He built more rooms to accommodate his patients for healing and convalescence. After the doctor sold it, several families stayed on the property for a short amount of time. Every time the house was traded from one family to the next, the state of disrepair worsened. Lynn Pirozzoli purchased the property in 1992 and restored it to its former glory. In March 2019, Martlet Holdings of Charlottesville purchased the inn.

After walking through the downstairs area, I headed upstairs to take a few pictures and get some recordings. Climbing the stairs on the far side of the entryway, I was hoping the Dancing Ghost would appear, but he didn't. He is heard late at night until early morning, tap-dancing at the top of the stairs.

All the rooms were simply stunning in their decor. Reynard's Retreat is done in fox-hunt themes. Hunter's Haven, another elegant room, is where I almost tripped, as guests have to step down to enter it.

Entering the Burgundy Room, I stated out loud that if anyone wanted to say hello, they should feel free. Returning home and listening to the recording, I heard someone said, "hi!" right after I spoke. I was by myself in the hallway. Looking for a small impression on the bed, I was excited to find one. This male ghost likes to leave an impression on the bedspread, especially after the housekeepers have made the bed for the day.

Left: One of the entities at Black Horse Inn loves to tap dance on the stairs late at night.

Below: The Burgandy Room bed, where if you look closely, you will see a small impression where someone seems to have sat after the bed was made.

The Garden Room came next, and it is just as nice as its counterpart rooms. I felt a twinge and cold chills, but nothing else. The Rosemont had a four-poster canopy bed done in red velvet but no activity that I could determine. The Jeffersonian had many Thomas Jefferson antiques and artifacts and was a favorite of mine, though no activity was noted.

After taking pictures upstairs, I met Michelle once more to get some historical information about the inn. Michelle was telling some guests about the front two rooms and how they were used as a hospital in the war. There is also a story about the Laughing Nurse, who tries to cheer up her patients. She is heard mostly by male guests and is usually in the oldest part of the inn late at night.

The nurse was first heard by a contractor who didn't believe in ghosts. One night, he went running up the stairs, looking very pale and searching for the owner. He asked the owner if she had just been downstairs laughing or making any noise. The owner told him she had been painting in another part of the house all day. He immediately left and never worked past dark again.

Finally, there is the aforementioned Scrooge. After three years of his antics, the owner finally told him what she thought of his mischievous shenanigans. She also made sure to start securing the Christmas tree on hooks with twine to prevent any more accidents.

Black Horse Inn (closed in 2022)
8393 Meetze Road
Warrenton, VA 20187
540-349-4020
https://www.virginia.org/listing/black-horse-inn/9710/

5

ORANGE & CHARLOTTESVILLE

INN AT WILLOW GROVE

Nestled in the Blue Ridge foothills, this historic inn has grown since it was first built in 1778. Currently, seven rooms with private baths are offered to guests. Dinner is served Thursdays through Sundays in a quaint dining area. Guests can take a walk behind the property for an amazing view of the mountains against the valley below.

Both Revolutionary War and Civil War soldiers camped on the property and used the site to set up headquarters for commanding officers. Be careful when exploring, as there are deep trenches on the grounds where soldiers hid during the wars.

With an inn steeped in the history of two wars, it seems apropos that a few restless spirits roam the property. One legend states that an African American woman walks the hallways with her two children fathered by a former property owner. The man decided to have them all killed, and they were buried on the grounds in unmarked graves.

A younger couple is seen in the parlor either late at night or in the early morning. Reports of voices and people walking the stairs and hallways are not uncommon. Perhaps the most common occurrence is guests seeing two Confederate soldiers resting under the large trees by the driveway.

The couple who owned the inn was changing clothes one night and left their garments over the back of a chair. The next morning, the clothes were

Inn at Willow Grove.

gone. No one had entered the room all night. Finally, several weeks later, the clothes showed up, having been washed and folded.

Inn at Willow Grove
14079 Plantation Way
Orange, VA 22960
540-317-1206
https://www.innatwillowgrove.com/

Lafayette Inn

Located in Stanardsville, Virginia, this unique inn is known for its scrumptious ice cream. When I visited the location, several people stood in line to sample the tasty treat. This historic landmark, built in a Federal style in 1840 by Robert Pritchett, includes a dining room on the lower level and a wraparound porch. Innkeepers Alan and Kaye Pyles traveled far and wide before deciding to open the Lafayette Inn. While traveling, they spent their time figuring out how to best run their own establishment and what pleased them the most as guests. Five rooms are available, named for former presidents. The Dicey Cottage is named for an enslaved person who lived there.

Guests can see the edge of the property, where the original slave quarters were located. An office and small kitchen are housed in the back building,

Lafayette Inn.

which was used as a stable at one time. The inn served as various businesses in its history, such as a restaurant, a saloon and a hospital during the Civil War. The basement housed the hospital for the soldiers, and it is believed that many died from typhoid fever during the war.

Hauntings have occurred over the years at the Lafayette. Under one rug, there is a bloodstain that keeps returning, no matter how many times it is scrubbed away. Apparently, a Confederate soldier committed suicide when he found out about his wife's affair. He is still seen walking the hallways, ready to shoot the Yankee soldier with a pistol at his side.

The inn is also home to a whole feral community that is as cute as can be. The menagerie includes ten cats, one set of triplet kittens and one raccoon. Check out the gorgeous creatures on their website (www.thelafayette.com/feralfamily). Consider this a quick public service announcement to help out the sweet creatures.

Lafayette Inn
146 Main Street
Stanardsville, VA 22973
434-985-6345
https://www.thelafayette.com

HOLLYMEAD HOUSE (FORMERLY SILVER THATCH INN)

Located off Route 29 in Charlottesville, Hollymead House (formerly Silver Thatch Inn) is a colonial farmhouse boasting seven rooms named after presidents born in Virginia. A restaurant with three separate dining areas is enjoyed by not only the paying guests but also the public. Counted among one of the oldest structures in Central Virginia, it is not too far from other popular and older attractions, such as Michie Tavern (haunted), Monticello (haunted) and the Blue Ridge Parkway. The owners, Pamela and William Calary, want to give their guests a true vacation. There are no phones or televisions in the rooms, giving people a chance to "unplug" from their troubles, if only for a little while.

The location originally served as a Native American reservation. It became a jail in 1780 for Hessian soldiers captured by General Horatio Gates while the American Revolution raged. The wings to the elegant inn, added in 1912 and 1937, brought an opportunity for more commercial growth. (B.F.D. Runk, dean of University of Virginia, added a wing.) The center part of the building provided the room for a boys' school in 1812, and the surrounding land brought farming opportunities (melons and tobacco). At one time, the property consisted of almost three hundred acres. Now the inn sits on just one and a half acres.

Knowing that the Hessian Room is so named because of the jail formerly located in the same place, it is not surprising that some guests see Hessian soldiers walking around that part of the inn. Paranormal investigators have

Hollymead House (formerly Silver Thatch Inn).

visited and found many unique occurrences. One met a seven-foot-tall figure who stood behind one of the other investigators. They left quickly, thinking the figure didn't want to be bothered. One of the former owners at the time stated that they sometimes see a figure crawling across the stairs on the top level. No one knows what to make of these entities, but it is thought that Hessian soldiers from the war are still marching and training.

Terri Petrovits, a former owner, called in Twisted Paranormal Society to do an investigation. One member of the group, who is also a medium, headed up to the attic, where she saw a rather large figure who she estimated to be seven feet tall.

Another group headed to the Jefferson Room, employed as a dormitory in the 1800s. This room is considered a hot spot, so the group hoped to capture some recordings. A third group went to the Hessian Room, the oldest part of the building. There have been numerous reports from guests about activity in this room as well.

Some guests say their pillows are stolen by a Hessian soldier late at night. Disembodied voices are heard, and there is a spirit that climbs the stairs, only to sit down in a chair with a long sigh. One guest heard the floorboards squeak in her room, as though someone was walking across them, but when she investigated, she found that she was alone in the room. In the Jefferson Room, one guest awoke to see an apparition move across the room. The guest watched curiously for a while and then went back to sleep. He said that he didn't think the figure was malevolent. There is an older family graveyard on the grounds that may contain some of the entities who still roam the inn.

Hollymead House (Formerly Silver Thatch Inn)
3001 Hollymead Drive
Charlottesville, VA 22911
813-362-2954
https://www.hollymeadhouse.com

Inn at Court Square

The best way to locate the Inn at Court Square is to look for a bright-red door. It was the first thing I noticed about one of the oldest buildings in Charlottesville. Edward Butler built the five-room structure in 1785. Opie Norris took it over in 1808. Known as the Butler-Norris House, it held other

Inn at Court Square.

businesses, such as a real estate brokerage, law firm and slate company, as well as a church.

Today, two houses make up the inn: the Butler-Norris House and the Molly Johnson House. There are ten exquisite rooms for guests to enjoy, complete with private bathrooms and fireplaces. On the lower level, guests can peruse DeLoach Antiques, an eclectic mix of midcentury pieces throughout the inn that are also for sale.

Ghost stories go hand-in-hand with the inn due to its age and the eighteenth-century architecture that takes you back to those days. A favorite story of one of the owners, Candace DeLoach, is that of a porter named John who worked at the inn and carried guests' luggage to their rooms. A three-candle sconce hung on the wall near the bottom of the stairs. When John transported luggage up the stairs, he would inevitably knock the sconce off the wall. He tried telling the owner to move it elsewhere, but it stayed in its original spot. After John passed away, strange happenings began taking place. Once, the owner felt something fly past her. When she investigated what it was, it turned out to be a candle from the sconce. No one else was near the sconce or the stairs at the time.

One year later, another unusual occurrence took place. Water began running from a spot that had previously been fixed. A plumber came to fix the problem, and he found that some nails had punctured the water pipe. The last time the wall had been opened up was two years before that. Ms. DeLoach said it seemed as if someone had pushed the nails through the pipe. She decided to take John's funeral eulogy and place it in the wall where the problem was. They never had another issue with the wall.

Other entities are seen from time to time in the upstairs rooms. One guest saw a doctor in military dress standing beside her bed. He disappeared when she screamed. Another guest saw a lady wearing period clothing.

Inn at Court Square
410 East Jefferson Street
Charlottesville, VA 22902
434-295-2800
http://www.innatcourtsquare.com

6

HARRISONBURG, STAUNTON & NELSON

By the Side of the Road Getaway Lodging

Looking at this large, white house standing by a lazy pond, it seems like an idyllic place to spend time away from the world. Built in 1789 by Samuel Miller, the house was used to support the Mennonite community in the surrounding area. Miller had migrated to Harrisonburg from Pennsylvania and was an active leader in the local church. His son, Micah, took the house after Samuel died.

During the Civil War, a Union sympathizer, John B. Wegner, bought the house. Since Mennonites were pacifists, they tended to be against any kind of conflict. The house was employed as a makeshift Civil War hospital. It also provided shelter and served as a hiding place for Union soldiers and supporters from the Confederate army.

In 1864, Union General Philip Sheridan received his orders to enter the Shenandoah Valley and burn all Confederate properties and crops. He tried to burn the inn as well. He was angry at the fact that a group of Confederate soldiers dressed in Union gear had killed some of his officers without giving them the chance to surrender first. He set out to destroy the whole area, burning seventeen houses and five barns. This particular incident was called Burning of the Valley.

After many homeowners lost their own property due to fires, they settled at the inn. Sheridan tried to burn it down several times, but the inside walls

By the Side of the Road Getaway Lodging.

were built with fire-resistant bricks. As the house survived the burning attempts, it became even more of a focal point for the Mennonite community. One bishop, Peter Burkholder, even dared to preach to his German-speaking followers in English. Rumor has it that some of the soldiers from the hospital would steal pies from a neighboring home.

Janice and Dennis Fitzgerald purchased the property in 1998 and converted it into Harrisonburg's first bed-and-breakfast, complete with three private cottages. They also included a mini-kitchen in each room to allow meals to be made in the room. A delicious gourmet breakfast can also be delivered every morning.

A cemetery sits behind the main house. Individuals interred here include early inhabitants of the inn and their families, Civil War soldiers and Harrisonburg leaders. Because of the cemetery and the well-known history, many say the inn is haunted. Apparently, footsteps are heard on the third floor at odd hours of the night by guests. After asking the owners about the late-night movements, guests say they never left their room.

It is also thought that the B&B is haunted by two former owners and their little girl. One night, the innkeepers were expecting their daughter to arrive at the inn. They heard the front door open and footsteps making their way to the family. When their daughter didn't show up in the room, they went looking for her and found no one. She showed up about an hour later and knew nothing about the previous incident. Guests say you can sometimes hear the daughter still trying to sneak back in during the late hours of the night.

Doors open and close by themselves; some guests think it may be the Civil War soldiers who came to the location when it offered medical care for the wounded. Some guests hear ghostly conversation outside their rooms, but they never find anyone there.

By the Side of the Road Getaway Lodging
491 Garbers Church Road
Harrisonburg, VA 22801
540-801-0430
https://www.bythesideoftheroad.com

Ubon Thai Victorian Restaurant Inn

Located not far from Mary Baldwin College, the Ubon Thai Inn (formerly the Belle Grae Inn) is a quaint location with a restaurant and four guest rooms. Originally a seventeen-room mansion done in Italian Victorian style, the rooms held many amenities, such as coffee makers and fireplaces. Michael Organ, owner and operator of Belle Grae Inn for close to thirty years, sold the property in the fall of 2010. Ubon Herlong bought the property at auction and opened her famous Thai restaurant. It serves many delicacies to guests, including crispy pork, crispy fish, yellow curry and panang curry.

In the early 1800s, a guest checked in and now refuses to leave. Her favorite spot was Room 7. Mischievous at times, she will unlock the guest room doors. If she decides she doesn't like a guest, she will make the hot water supply bypass the room, and the guest gets a chilling awakening in the morning. One guest said they felt the bed vibrating at some point during the night and that something touched their arm.

For presidential history buffs, Woodrow Wilson, the twenty-eighth president of the United States, was born just a few blocks down, at 24 North Coalter Street. He also has a room memorialized for him at the University of Virginia on the West Range (Room 31). (Incidentally, Edgar Allan Poe's Room is 13.) The Woodrow Wilson Birthplace and Presidential Library is in Staunton, Virginia (www.woodrowwilson.org). Wilson's room at the University of Virginia is in Charlottesville (https://range.student.virginia.edu/jeffersonian-project). Ubon Thai Inn has four rooms at present for guests, and the location was closed when I visited.

Ubon Thai Victorian Restaurant and Inn (Formerly Belle Grae Inn)
(closed in 2021)
515 West Frederick Street
Staunton, VA 24401
540-886-4141
http://www.ubonthaivictorian.com

Ubon Thai Restaurant Inn.

MARK ADDY INN

This unique bed-and-breakfast may be off the beaten path, but that doesn't stop the owners from offering a relaxing getaway. Hang out in the parlor reading a good book or take a nature walk around the grounds.

Built by Charles Everett in the 1800s, the property formerly consisted of one log cabin. Thomas Jefferson was a good friend and invited Everett to be his personal physician. Everett remained childless, but he had one favorite nephew, John, who followed in his footsteps and became a doctor. John did have one strike against him in Everett's book: he owned many slaves. To make John see the wrong in this practice, Everett left very specific wording in his will. John wanted the house that Everett built, but he could have it on one condition: He had to free all of his slaves. John refused and received the Upland Farm instead. (John's son John Coleman married Nellie Martin, the first postmistress of Lodebar. Nellysford, Virginia, was named for her.)

John and Nellie renovated the house, adding seven rooms for all of their children. As a result, many descendants still live in Nelson County, and they like to visit the inn every so often to relive old memories.

John Maddox purchased the property in the 1990s and renamed it in honor of his grandparents Mark and Adelaide. When asked about strange occurrences at the inn, he said he always felt there was something present, but he never saw anything. He said that the room at the top of the stairs had some activity. This is the same room where I felt a strong pull during my tour of the inn. Currently, Leslie and Rafael Tal run the charming inn, which makes for an excellent vacation spot.

While exploring the property, I took in all the charm and history of the location. The façade is a bright blue and yellow with a working fountain out in front of the inn. Inside, you will find elegant rooms and a restaurant for delicious meals during your stay. There are many animals to meet as well. A guest favorite is the twenty-three-year-old parrot Baby who occupies the middle space of the parlor. Several dogs and cats roam the property, but all seem to be very sweet and welcoming.

I asked about hauntings and if any had occurred for the present owners. Jen, one of the staff, saw a lady standing by the lamppost outside one night while she was walking her dog. The dog managed to get loose, and Jen had to chase after him. She noticed the woman standing by the lamppost and waved, thinking it was a guest getting some fresh air. Jen got no response from the lady, only an ominous stare. Later, she asked some of the

Mark Addy Inn.

other guests if they knew the red-headed lady; no one had seen her before that night.

Some guests have told stories of other happenings. Some hear people walking the halls at night. When they open the door to see who is out there, they find no one. They also have a problem with pictures slanting. The pictures, located in the Rue de Monet Room, refuse to hang straight. Guests discovered this after trying to straighten them. The next morning, they were hanging at an angle again. It is believed that Nellie Martin is causing the pictures to go askew.

Jen has seen an older gentleman appear in the kitchen at different times of the day. Pictures taken throughout the house show orbs and different lights. One of the security cameras caught a floating orb that traveled down the stairs and through the house. Despite these occurrences, the owners say the house has a good vibe to it and that there is no malevolence.

There are two rooms here where people passed away. The owners discovered that a doctor owned the house in the past. It thus behooved the sick to visit him for treatment. One room was described as having a heavy feeling, but after renovations, it became much lighter. The owner told me that a little girl roams in one of the rooms. They believe she may be an Everett family child who died of appendicitis.

I experienced a strong pull to the Colonel Room, at the top of the stairs and a strong presence throughout the room. (This is the room that John Maddox also thought had a presence.) Others have found hot spots on the staircase and in some rooms on the second floor.

The Mimosa Room has a mischievous entity that turns the bathroom faucets on and off. It has been discovered that when the housekeepers are cleaning, the entity will constantly turn on the water, even after someone has made sure the handle is shut off tight.

The Elena Room has the reputation of having the squeakiest floors in the building. As we walked across them, they creaked horribly. The interesting thing about this room is that it has its own balcony connecting to the original front porch, which sits on the right side of the house if you are outside facing it.

The Schloss Room has a spirit that turns the lights on and off. Guests have seen the light turn on while they are outside, and the lights will turn on after the guests turn them off before they go to sleep. When guests wake up in the middle of the night, the lights are burning bright.

There are pictures of one entity on the property. The spirit was first seen in a photograph taken during a wedding, looking out the window as if watching the ceremony.

Lamppost where Jen saw a lady staring at her when she was trying to catch her dog.

Colonel Room. Is that a ghost showing up in the mirror on the left side?

Guests who are looking for a nice, quiet getaway with plenty to see and do will find that this is the right place. There may even be an extra guest hiding in the shadows.

Mark Addy Inn (closed in 2023 for renovations)
56 Rodes Farm Drive
Nellysford, VA 22958
434-361-1101
https://www.mark-addy.com

7

HOT SPRINGS, ROANOKE & ABINGDON

OMNI HOMESTEAD RESORT

Located on some two thousand acres of the Allegheny Mountains, this resort has much to offer in the way of charm and hospitality. It has been a welcoming destination to over twenty U.S. presidents, and the spa carries the same mineral waters that Thomas Jefferson enjoyed in 1818. Amenities include a spa and salon, several pools and a lazy river, a fitness center, snow tubing, eighteen-hole golf and a zip line tour. For those who like to explore, there are a number of breweries, antiques shops, art galleries and shopping plazas within six miles of the resort. There is something for everyone in this quaint town. The location has been named a National Historic Landmark.

Native Americans lived on these lands before they were developed by European surveyors and explorers. The Native Americans knew that the waters in the Hot Springs area had rejuvenating powers and used the site for healing the sick.

The first surveyors who happened across the area were Thomas Bullitt and Charles and Andrew Lewis. In 1764, Bullitt and the Lewis brothers paid thirty shillings for three hundred acres, which included the natural hot springs. Two years later, the eighteen-room hotel was built and opened as the Homestead, named for homesteaders who helped to build it and the bathhouses on the surrounding property. Bullitt owned the historic resort until he died at home in 1778 during the American Revolutionary War. The deed stayed in his family until 1832.

Omni Homestead Resort.

A prominent physician, Dr. Thomas Goode, acquired the resort in 1832 and brought the European spa treatments to guests. After he died in 1858, his family decided to keep the resort. A prominent lawyer moved to the region in 1881. M.E. Ingalls, looking to extend lines for the Chesapeake and Ohio Railway, researched the area to find where lines could be added to make travel faster and more efficient. Ingalls bought the Homestead in 1888 with several other investors, including J.P. Morgan, who wanted to build up the area around the resort. Within a year, they had raised the financing (more than $1 million) to build a fancier hotel.

Disaster struck on July 2, 1901, when a fire broke out and burned the entire building. The following year, the resort was reopened with a new wing and one more to be completed. M.E. Ingalls died in 1914, but his family had retained possession of the resort since 1911. They added many new rooms, including the Crystal, Garden and Empire Rooms, in the early 1920s. They also added a theater and a tower in the late 1920s. During World War II, the hotel served as an internment camp for Japanese diplomats. The Garden Wing was completed in 1973.

Other additions to the already lavish resort included the grounds for two golf courses, tennis, horseback riding, skiing, snow tubing and fly-fishing. Skiing became popular in 1959, when the first slopes opened. The hotel also incorporated two pools and a lazy river with a children's play zone in 2012.

The grand resort has also had its share of famous visitors through the years. Thomas Jefferson soaked in the rejuvenating waters near the resort, the Duchess and Duke of Windsor (Wallis Simpson and Prince Edward, formerly King Edward VIII) stayed for a month and Woodrow Wilson spent his honeymoon at the resort. Other presidents who visited include James

Madison, Dwight Eisenhower, William McKinley, William Taft (who spent two months in 1908), Richard Nixon, Gerald Ford, Jimmy Carter, Ronald Reagan, George H.W. Bush and Bill Clinton. Pro golfer and tour champion Sam Snead not only grew up in the surrounding area, but he also worked as a golf pro at the resort for many decades.

There are rumors of a haunting within the walls of this famed resort. In the early twentieth century, a wedding was to set commence. The groom got cold feet and left the bride at the altar. After searching for him for many years, she finally died of heartbreak. Guests and staff alike say they have seen her walking the halls, asking what time it is. She is waiting for the exact minute when her love will return and marry her. In another story, she roams the fourteenth floor, asking anyone she happens upon for the time. She is hoping to meet the groom at the altar at the correct time. It also said that she committed suicide when he didn't return following their wedding day.

Omni Homestead Resort
7696 Sam Snead Highway
Hot Springs, VA 24445
540-839-1766
https://www.omnihotels.com/hotels/homestead-virginia

Natural Bridge Hotel

Located in Rockbridge County, the Natural Bridge Hotel sits high on a hill and is a destination for travelers from all over the globe. The tall columns and architecture only add to its charm.

For twenty shillings in 1774, Thomas Jefferson purchased the land, 157 acres, from King George III. Jefferson built himself a log cabin with two rooms, one for houseguests. Many interesting people stayed with him, including James Monroe, Henry Clay and Martin Van Buren. Guests could explore the beautiful countryside on horseback or by horse-drawn carriages.

Colonel Henry Parsons owned the resort in the 1880s. Around 1890, the owners moved up the hill to the present-day location and built the main hotel, known then as the Appledore. The name changed to the Natural Bridge Hotel in the early 1900s. Tragedy struck in April 1963, when the hotel caught on fire. No one knows what caused the blaze, but reports say it may have started in the kitchen.

Natural Bridge Hotel. *Courtesy of Michael Schwartz.*

Reconstruction started in 1964 under the watchful eye of James N. Hunter, and the doors opened again to guests in 1965. Sadly, Hunter committed suicide in 1976 (general manager, 1945–76). The venue has flourished since that time and is known for its great amenities and wedding planning.

An old legend concerns a former owner of the hotel. He apparently went mad one night and killed his family at the hotel. Apparitions of his wife and children can be seen walking in the hallways.

One employee told me a story about a front desk phone that rings at odd hours. The caller ID indicates that the call is from the building across the street, formerly a wax museum. The only problem is that there is no phone in that building at present.

Other phenomena have occurred as well. One guest heard someone walking on the floor above her, even though she was staying on the top floor. Another guest said that she saw a glowing figure in her room in the middle of the night. The figure, which appeared to be a Native American, sat unmoving on the floor for some time. Some guests complain about children running up and down the hallways throughout the day and night. They open the door to tell them to quiet down and find nobody outside their door and the corridor empty.

Other guests recounted something trying to pull the sheet off them during the night. One lost his socks, and when he returned to his room, they were sitting on the end of his bed. A female traveler opened one of the ghost apps she had downloaded to her phone to see if she could find anything. The word *ice* appeared. At that same time, her sister was refilling their cooler.

For added adventure, be sure to check out the Natural Bridge Formation, located about three minutes from the hotel (www.naturalbridgestatepark. org). A 215-foot limestone arch, it was thought to be sacred to the Monacan Natives before being seen in the 1700s by European explorers. Not only is it a Virginia landmark, but it is also considered to be a natural wonder.

Natural Bridge Hotel
15 Appledore Lane
Natural Bridge, VA 24578
540-291-2121
https://www.naturalbridgeva.com.

PATRICK HENRY HOTEL

Located in downtown Roanoke, this hotel was built in the Colonial Revival style. Designed by William Stoddart in 1925, the Patrick Henry Hotel opened in November with more than two thousand people in attendance. The name for the hotel, determined through a contest, came from John Payne, who starred in *Miracle on 34th Street* and decided on Patrick Henry, Virginia's first governor.

The Patrick Henry offered both apartments and hotel rooms through the late 1980s. A $3 million renovation was completed in 1990 by Affirmative Equities of New York. By the late 1990s, the firm considered turning the hotel into senior apartments. Twice, these attempts failed to come to fruition. The location was condemned as not compliant with current fire code. In late 2010, the Jefferson College of Health Sciences reserved 56 units for incoming students. Today, it comprises more than 130 apartments and event spaces. You can still walk through the lobby and see the ornate fixtures. Timothy Kaine, former governor of Virginia, has an office in the lobby.

Entering through the front door, I was amazed to see the beautiful lobby and high-rise ceiling. Knowing three gentleman ghosts haunt the ballroom, I headed to the second floor. Running into some caterers for a wedding that was taking place that afternoon, I asked about the hotel and any interesting occurrences. Several of the caterers stated that this would be the place for a haunting. Asking to visit the ballroom for some pictures, I felt a hard twinge walking through the ballroom door.

Patrick Henry Hotel.

After I left the ballroom, I asked if any other areas would be of interest, and another caterer said that the downstairs area is really haunted. There is a bar there at present. It was not open, but one can ask the manager to go down there.

Research shows that a well-known ghost still roams the location. Miss Lucy has been seen wearing a long white dress at least forty times by other guests. Many of the return guests, such as pilots and flight attendants, know the story and request the room Miss Lucy likes to haunt in the early morning hours. She stays near to the one where she lived and died, according to a former manager.

Haunted ballroom where three gentlemen ghosts like to roam.

One guest ran from the room after seeing a staircase appear out of nowhere and a lady come down the stairs and walk across the room.

People have also seen lights turn on and off by themselves and cold spots in the hallways, coupled with unexplained footsteps. No explanation can ever be found. Several EVPs have been taken in the hotel, revealing conversations about the people who used to live there. An apparition of an older gentleman with a pipe has been seen on the second floor. He sits at a table and will start kicking the tablecloth with his foot to get your attention.

The most active room is believed to be 606. An airline attendant was stabbed and left in the room's bathtub. Her killer was never caught. Some guests who spend the night in the room say they watch the ghost of the stewardess reach down from the ceiling to touch them while they are lying in bed.

Room 1017 belonged to a numerologist in her seventies. She was a bit of a recluse, and her body was not discovered for a couple of weeks after she died of unknown causes. Her room could not be rented even more than twenty years later because of the smell of death. Her passing was thought to be not peaceful, as some guests claimed to hear faint moaning and screaming. The smell would become so strong that guests would have to leave in order to breathe.

Patrick Henry Hotel
611 South Jefferson Street
Roanoke, VA 24011
540-491-9558
https://thepatrickhenry.com

Hotel Roanoke

Built by the Norfolk & Western Railroad (N&W) in 1882, this Tudor-style hotel contained about thirty-five rooms for its guests. It was nicknamed the "Grand Old Lady" because of its original Queen Anne style before renovation. The hotel offered a perfect blend of the past and excellent hospitality, and people in the railroad business and travelers alike were drawn to the mountain air of the location.

During the Great Depression, N&W spent over $220,000 to add a seventy-five-room wing and modern features, such as movable telephones, electric fans and ice water. A major fire broke out in 1935, and this led to a complete renovation in 1938. It closed from 1989 to 1995 and went through another remodeling. The hotel returned to its former glory, with antiques throughout the lobby and in the Pine Room, where officers congregated during World War II. In addition, the number of guest rooms reached more than 330. Flashing back to its railroad history, the hotel features specific train services on the website (www.hotelroanoke.com/virginias_blue_ridge/amtrak_virginia/ or www.hotelroanoke.com/virginia_hotel_deals/Train_Lovers_Package).

The Renew Roanoke campaign in 1992 brought more than $7 million to facilitate another restoration and the addition of a pedestrian bridge and a conference center. The hotel reopened in 1995 and had the distinct honor of being placed on the Virginia Historical Landmark list, complete with a marker near the main entrance. Guests who stay at the hotel are in great company. Some of the more famous guests have included six presidents (from Eisenhower to Bush 41, Wayne Newton, George Takei, Aerosmith, Thomas Edison and Henry Ford). Along with all the new touches, the owners also wanted to leave a little bit of nostalgia for returning guests. The original ceiling in the Palm Court still renders the constellations, a feature that was

Hotel Roanoke.

present when the first train arrived in Roanoke in 1852. Take time to view the surrounding area.

Josh, an employee at Natural Bridge Hotel, told some stories about this location. A former general manager who just happened to be CEO for the Norfolk-Southern Railway lived on one of the upper floors of the hotel. He turned the suite into a small apartment and wound up hanging himself in the room. After a series of fires and major renovations to the hotel, management decided to block the suite off so that no one could gain access to it. Josh said that it is quite eerie on the fifth floor whenever he has to go.

One guest woke up at 3:00 a.m. every night, saying that there was a strange vibe in her room. One person I spoke to at another hotel said they had previously stayed at the Hotel Roanoke. They had also been awakened by noises in the hallway and people walking down the corridor. When they opened their door to ask them to be quiet, no one was there. The hotel has a book in which guests can write of any spooky happenings that occur. Be sure to see what new things may have occurred recently. This is a great read for those looking for other ghost sightings in the hotel.

Hotel Roanoke
110 Shenandoah Avenue NE
Roanoke, VA 24016
540-985-5900
https://www.hotelroanoke.com

Blacksburg Holiday Inn

The Blacksburg Holiday Inn is closed now, but I still included this location in these pages, as it has been said to be a hot spot for hauntings and other happenings. From the accompanying picture, visitors can see that there is another hotel-type building behind the main strip mall, so it may still be possible to catch an EVP or get a picture. As always, ask first.

The Blacksburg Holiday Inn was built on an old plantation site. Jacob Harman, who was first to settle the area, would hang his lantern to mark where Native Americans crossed the New River. The property became known as "Jacob's Lantern Plantation."

Employees noticed disembodied voices, loud music and laughing long after the hotel nightclub closed for the night. Managers even reported that

Former location of the Blacksburg Holiday Inn.

ghostly guests asked that the volume of the loud music be lowered, even though no music was playing at the time.

Blacksburg Holiday Inn (former site)
900 Prices Fork Road
Blacksburg, VA 24060

MARTHA WASHINGTON INN & SPA

Located in Abingdon, Virginia, the Martha Washington Inn was built by General Francis Preston for his wife, Sarah Buchanan Preston, and their nine children in 1832 at a cost of $15,000. The family lived in the home until 1858, when it was purchased by the founders of Martha Washington College. The women's college, named after the first First Lady, operated until 1928.

Martha Washington Inn. *Courtesy of Don Molnar (Haunted M.D.).*

After the Civil War broke out in 1861, some events that occurred at the college may have led to the hauntings. Not only did the college serve as a place to train Confederate soldiers, but it also served as a hospital for the sick and injured. Many students at the college became nurses and took care of soldiers admitted to their wards.

In the early 1900s, typhoid fever became so widespread that it affected one hundred out of every one hundred thousand people. Since there were few working sewage systems, food and water became diseased from people already sick or carriers of the disease.

The 1930s brought the Great Depression, and some students left or didn't enroll because of the rapidly declining economy. The school closed for good in 1932. For many years after, the Barter Theater (also haunted) began using the location as housing for its performers. Many well-known actors got their start here, including Ned Beatty, Patricia Neal and Ernest Borgnine. In 1935, the Martha Washington Inn opened, welcoming guests from all over the globe. Many other famous names have stayed at the charming inn, including Harry Truman, Jimmy Carter, Eleanor Roosevelt and Elizabeth Taylor.

Luckily, many aspects of the inn have been saved from the damage of time. The main lobby used to be the living room of the original Preston family home. The parlors and the grand staircase remain as they were in the 1800s. The grandfather clock, a rare Dutch Baroque item from England, now stands in the Edith Wilson Parlor.

A renovation and restoration came in 1984, costing millions of dollars. The owners wanted to preserve the original details as much as possible. The hotel stands as a gateway to history as well as a modern-day establishment. It is listed in Historic Hotels of America under the National Trust for Historic Preservation.

With all this rich history, it seems natural that this particular site would have a few hauntings. There seems to be plenty of activity throughout the hotel. It is considered one of the most haunted hotels in Virginia.

Beth, who attended Martha Washington College, tried her best to nurse a sick soldier, Captain John Stoves, back to health. He always requested that she play a melody on her violin for him while he rested. While she cared for him, they fell in love. He passed away, and Beth died three weeks later of typhoid fever. They are buried together in a nearby cemetery. If you listen closely on the third floor, you may still be able to hear Beth playing her violin. Some have seen her apparition in the room as well. Other stories have this same event happening in other places in the hotel, such as in Room 217 or Room 403.

There is a story about a Confederate soldier taking some documents to General Robert E. Lee regarding the location of the Union army. He wanted to say goodbye to his girlfriend before he left. He tried to sneak into her dorm at Martha Washington College using the underground cave system. Caught by Union soldiers, he was killed in front of his girlfriend. The stain from his spilled blood remains outside the Governor's Room, even after many changes of carpet. The carpeting always has unexplained holes or stains, so hotel management switched to a wooden floor.

Sometimes in the hallways, you might see a trail of mud going down the corridor. Apparently, a soldier using a crutch to walk limps on his way. This particular hallway on the third floor is also said to be an active cold spot.

Enslaved persons were once kept in the basement of the inn. Some people have encountered what they think is a tormented entity down there from Civil War days.

An injured Union soldier came to the makeshift hospital during the war to receive medical attention. The horse he rode to reach the location is still seen roaming the grounds of the inn, waiting to take the soldier back to his camp.

A very irate spirit appears in the tunnel that leads from the inn to Barter Theatre (www.bartertheatre.com). The passageway collapsed on the gentleman in 1890 as he was walking through to the other side. Actors and guests who use the walkway can feel his anger, even in the dark. The tunnel has been said to give off a malevolent feeling by some people who have visited it. No one knows the identity of the spirit.

Good friends Don Molnar and Christine Day visited the hotel and sent me some interesting notes about it. Checking into Room 214, they had no idea that it was in one of the most haunted hallways. Civil War soldiers were treated at the hospital in this part of the property. Don stated that activity was rampant in the room, as evidenced from readings by the equipment he brought with him for the investigation, including K2 meters, a parascope, a motion light that activated when something was nearby and his SLS camera, which shows stick figures on the screen of entities in the room.

The guests next door in Room 215 reported that some things were tossed across their room, including a lamp that crashed to the floor. At some point during the night, they packed and left rather hastily. A previous guest reported seeing an apparition of a lady in Room 217, which is where one story has Beth playing the violin.

On the first evening, Don and Christine walked through the hotel taking pictures to see if they could capture anything. In one photo taken from the older part looking across to a newer wing, there appears to be a soldier in the window. Perhaps it is General Preston watching over his beloved home. (The gentleman looks like he is wearing glasses and a surgeon's mask.) No one knows for sure, as the property housed both Confederate and Union soldiers.

There is a white gazebo with a black top located at the back of the hotel, and many guests have seen the ghosts of Civil War soldiers walking through the area. The phantom horse has also been seen here.

Don did his own investigating one night, taking an audio recorder and his SLS camera with him. He experienced the feeling of being watched in the hallway outside his room, the original part of the hotel, the library and the event rooms opposite the library. He

Ghost in window that looks like a gentleman standing in the top right corner of window. *Courtesy of Christine Day.*

actually caught some figures on his SLS camera in the area where he later learned a female ghost liked to roam. The library is known to have a globe that turns by itself. While Don didn't see that happen, he did notice some type of moving energy, based on the K2 meter he used.

Don received a tour of some places that guests normally don't visit, as the security guard knew he was a ghost hunter. They started off in the kitchen and headed down to a few levels underground. A dark shadow is known to haunt this area. Don also mentioned seeing the tunnel entrance that leads to the Barter Theatre, but he said it was closed now.

They went back upstairs to the main ballroom above the dining area in a newer part of the building. In one corner, Don discovered the most activity he had thus far seen, with some loud banging noises and many shadow figures. He also noticed a distinct heaviness about the room and heard a loud bang when a shadow figure disappeared from the camera's view.

They returned to the event rooms, and once again, Don caught a figure on the SLS camera. The guard became quiet and then told Don that it was the same area where guests have seen a female ghost.

Apparently, the hotel has a notebook that keeps track of ghostly happenings. Among the notations are the following: The third and fourth floors seemed very active; hallway around 214 is active, with several rooms having varying activity; lights and televisions turn on and off by themselves; and Room 403 is believed to have poltergeist activity along with violin music.

Don's room, 214, is believed to be haunted by a Confederate soldier. He stated that the room was peaceful but a little creepy. He made mention of someone hitting or knocking on the room door. When he opened it to see what they wanted, no one was there. He caught several figures on his SLS camera that actually followed commands. The audio recorder caught unexplained noises in the room. He set up cameras to record while he slept. One camera caught the motion light going off and on at the same time the K2 meter and parascope were being activated. He did say that through all this activity, he and Christine never once felt threatened.

Martha Washington Inn & Spa
150 West Main Street
Abingdon, VA 24210
276-628-3161
http://www.themartha.com

CONCLUSION

A re you ready to book your next hotel stay and ask for one of the haunted rooms? Make plans to investigate some of the locations within these chapters. Just have fun and go with the attitude of learning some history and seeing how it plays out in today's world. You may get something, or you may not. To be honest, I do not get a great picture or recording every time. Watch out for all the unique occurrences that may lead you to catch something interesting, especially that ghost hanging over your shoulder as you read this.

I would love to see your pictures of any location, especially if you found something that wasn't supposed to be there. Maybe you had an extra guest you didn't know came along. Please message me through my website (www.susanschwartzauthor.com).

Thanks so much for going on this journey with me. I hope you relish the traveling, the investigating and the ghosties as much as I do.

For more haunted places in Virginia, check out my other book, *Haunted Charlottesville and Surrounding Counties*. You may find some great locations to investigate near you, as the book covers twelve counties in Virginia in and around Charlottesville.

GHOST TOURS IN VIRGINIA

Abingdon Spirit Tours, 276-706-6093, https://visitabingdonvirginia.com/directory/abingdon-spirit-tours.

Adults Only Twilight Cemetery Tours (Smithfield), 757-357-3367, 14477 Benn's Church Boulevard, Smithfield, VA 23430, https://stlukesmuseum.org/product/twilight-cemetery-tours-adults-only

Alexandria Colonial Tours, 703-519-1749, .221 King Street #3, Alexandria, VA 22314, https:www.alexcolonialtours.com.

Alexandria Ghost Tour, 844-383-0460, 203 Strand Street, Alexandria, VA 22314, http://www.nightlyspirits.com.

Appalachian Ghost Walks, 423-743-9255, Po Box 153, Unicoi, TN 37692, https://www.appalachianghostwalks.com.

Axwild Tours (Williamsburg), 757-565-0311, 112 Thomas Nelson Lane, Williamsburg, VA 23185, https://www.axwildtours.com/public-tour.

Bacon's Castle Haunt Nights, 804-648-1889, 204 West Franklin Street, Richmond, VA 23220. https://preservationvirginia.org/events/bacons-castle-haunt-nights. The castle is located at 465 Bacons Castle Trail, Surry, VA 23883.

Belle Grove Plantation, 540-621-7340, 9221 Belle Grove Drive, King George, VA 22485, https://www.bellegroveplantation.com.

Black Raven Paranormal/Afton Mountain Bed & Breakfast, 540-280-1833, 10273 Rockfish Valley Highway, Afton, VA 22920, https://www.aftonmountain.com/news/ghosts-staunton-walking-tour.

DC Ghosts, 844-757-5657 or 1-202-810-0709, https://dcghosts.com.

DC Secrets & Scandals, 1-888-651-9785, https://www.viator.com/tours/washington-dc/dc-ghost-tour/d657-70686P1.

Eerie Nights Ghost Tour (Richmond), 804-597-9379, 100 North 17th Street, Richmond, VA 23219, https://www.eerienights.tours.

Exchange Hotel, 540-832-2944, 400 South Main Street, Gordonsville, VA 22942, https://www.theexchangehotelmuseum.org.

Floyd Ghost Tour, 540-230-4862, 203 South Locust Street, Floyd, VA 24091, http://www.strangetalesoffloydcounty.com/floyd-ghost-tour.html.

Fort Monroe, 757-637-7778, Building 83, 20 Ingalls Road, Fort Monroe, VA 23651, https://fortmonroe.org/?s=Ghost+Tour.

Fredericksburg Civil War Tours, 540-760-5450, 706 Caroline Street, 2nd floor, Fredericksburg, VA 22401, www.fxbgtours.com.

Ghost & Vampire Tours, 1-844-407-1795, https://getyourguide.com (138 different tours in Washington, D.C., and surrounding cities).

Ghost City Tours, 1-855-999-9026, https://www.ghostcitytours.com.

Ghost Doctors Washington DC/Northern VA Ghost Tours, 703-686-4564, Old Town Manassas, https://ghostdoctors.com/ghost-tours-virginia.

Ghosts of Staunton Walking Ghost Tours, 540-448-2743, https://visitstaunton.com/listing/ghosts-of-staunton.

Ghost Story Tour of Washington, 240-721-0031, https://www.historicstrolls.com.

Ghost Tour of Colonial Williamsburg, 757-598-1805, 424 West Duke of Gloucester Street, Williamsburg, VA 23185, https://colonialghosts.com.

Hallowed Ground Tours, 540-809-3918, PO Box 3882, Fredericksburg, VA 22402. http://www.hallowedgroundtours.com/tours.html.

Haunted Harrisonburg Ghost Tour, 540-315-4685, https://www.eventbrite.com/e/haunted-harrisonburg-ghost-tour-tickets-38457546557, http://facebook.com/HarrisonburgGhostTours.

Haunted Progressive Tour, 804-829-5121, 501 Shirley Plantation Road, Charles City, 23030, https://shirleyplantation.com/calendar-event/haunted-progressive-tour-shirley-berkeley-edgewood-plantations.

Haunting Tales—Lexington Ghost Tour, 540-464-2250, 17 South Randolph Street, Lexington, VA 24450, http://ghosttourlexingtonva.com.

Haunts of Richmond, 804-543-3189, 5 South Twentieth Street, Richmond, VA 23233, https://www.hauntsofrichmond.com.

Historic Williamsburg Tours, 888-965-7254, 101 Visitor Center Drive, Williamsburg, VA 23185, https://www.colonialwilliamsburg.org/events/haunted-williamsburg.

Histories & Haunts (Virginia Beach), 757-498-2127, https://www.historiesandhaunts.com.

Legends on Main Street: A Suffolk Ghost Tour, 757-514-4130, https://www.virginia.org/listing/legends-of-main-street%3A-a-suffolk-ghost-walk-2021-tours/17161.

Manassas Museum, 703-368-1873, 9431 West Street, Manassas, VA 20110, https://www.manassasmuseum.org.

Middleburg Ghost Tours, 540-836-3152, http://www.middleburgghostours.com.

National Nightmares Ghost Tours, 703-593-7846, 212 2nd Street SE, Washington, DC, 20003, http://wwwnationalnightmares.com.

Neptune Ghosts, 267-636-9658, 2402 Atlantic Avenue, Virginia Beach, VA 23451, http://www.neptuneghosts.com.

Nightly Spirits (DC), 844-678-8687 or 1-8-GHOST-TOUR, 1475 Pennsylvania Avenue NW, Washington, DC 20004, https://nightlyspirits.com/dc-tours/old-town-tours.

Occoquan Spirits, 703-357-3850, 408 Mill Street, Occoquan, VA 22125, http://www.occoquanspirits.com.

Olde Town Carriage Tours, 540-371-0094, 706 Caroline Street, 2nd floor, Fredericksburg, VA 22404, http://www.oldetowncarriages.com.

Original Ghost Tour (Williamsburg), 757-707-7144, https://www.theghosttour.com.

Petersburg Haunts Walking Tours, 907-310-5093, 15 West Bank Street, Petersburg, VA 23803, http://www.facebook.com/PetersburgHaunts.

Richmond Ghosts, https://rvaghosts.com.

RVA (Richmond) Hidden History Storytellers Tours, 804-362-8200, 209 North 25th Street, Richmond, VA 23223, https://rvahiddenhistory.com.

Spooks & Legends (Williamsburg), 757-604-9985, http://www.spooksandlegends.com.

Tell Me about It Tours (Charlottesville), 434-760-0525, https://tellmeaboutittours.com.

Virginia Beach Ghost Walk, 757-422-1587, 2401 Atlantic Avenue, Virginia Beach, VA 23451, https://virginiabeach.guide/business-listing/virginia-beach-surf-rescue-museum.

Yorktown Ghost Walks, 757-759-1320, 301 Main Street, Yorktown, VA 23690, http://www.yorktownghostwalks.com.

BIBLIOGRAPHY

Adams, D. "Historic Patrick Henry Hotel in Downtown Roanoke Checks Back In." *Roanoke Times*, October 27, 2009. https://www.roanoke.com.

Allstays. "Boxwood Inn Ghost Story." 2019. https://www.allstays.com.

———. "Chamberlin Ghost Story." 2019. https://www.allstays.com.

Argos Paranormal. *The Witching Hour—Ep. 1*. "Belle Grove Plantation, Port Conway." October 22, 2018 (video). YouTube. www.youtube.com.

Barton, M.A. "Hotel Monaco Sold, to Become The Alexandrian." 2016. Patch. https://patch.com.

Bed and Breakfast. "Haunted Inns." 2020. http://www.bedandbreakfast.com.

Bed Breakfast Home. "Belle-Grae Inn and Restaurant." 2011. http://www.bedbreakfasthome.com.

Belle Grae Inn. "History, Hauntings, and the Paranormal." Facebook, April 14, 2019. https://www.facebook.com.

Belle Grove Plantation. "Ghost Cats of Belle Grove Plantation." YouTube, January 13, 2017 (video). http://www.youtube.com/watch?v=zrTHnSdJFA8.

———. "Paranormal." https://www.bellegroveplantation.com.

———. "Return to Belle Grove: A Haunting Conversation." YouTube, March 28, 2019 (video). http://www.youtube.com/watch?v=Ly72PDJxAss.

Beth. "The History Behind This Remote Hotel in Virginia Is Both Eerie and Fascinating." Only in Your State, January 27, 2018. https://www.onlyinyourstate.com.

———. Personal communication with author. Richard Johnston Inn, February 22, 2020.

———. "Stay Overnight in the 169 Year-Old Black Horse Inn, an Allegedly Haunted Spot in Virginia." Only in Your State, September 21, 2019. https://www.onlyinyourstate.com.

Betsy. Personal communication with author. Richard Johnston Inn, February 22, 2020.

Billock, J. "Tips from Syfy's Ghost Hunters: How (and Where!) to See a Ghost." Yahoo, October 30, 2015. http://yahoo.com.

Boone, J. "Health Care Students Will Check into Former Patrick Henry Hotel." *Roanoke (VA) Times*, November 30, 2010. https://www.roanoke.com.

———. "Then and Now: Hotel Roanoke." Roanoker, May 2, 2018. https://theroanoker.com.

———. "Then and Now: Patrick Henry Hotel." Roanoker, March 7, 2018. https://theroanoker.com.

Boyd, Robert. "'Haunted' Cavalier Hotel Attracting Some Unexpected Guests." 13 News Now, October 31, 2018. https://www.13newsnow.com.

Breakfast Home. "Silver Thatch Inn." 2011. http://www.bedbreakfasthome.com.

By the Side of the Road. "About Us." https://www.bythesideoftheroad.com.

Cannon, J. "There's No Place like Homestead." *Charlotte Observer*, August 15, 2014.

Cavalier Hotel. "A Historic Virginia Beach Hotel That Carries on a Grand Tradition." http://www.cavalierhotel.com.

Celebrity Ghost Hunters. "Celebrity Ghost Hunters Search for Paranormal Activity at Mineral Inn." *Central Virginian* (Louisa, VA), April 4, 2018. https://www.thecentralvirginian.com.

Center for Paranormal Research and Investigation. "Report: Chiswell Buck Trout Kitchen in Williamsburg, Va." September 1, 2005. https://centerpri.org.

Chou, K., and K. Robinson. "10 Real-Life Haunted Hotels That You Can Actually Stay In." *Town and Country*, October 5, 2021. https://www.townandcountrymag.com.

Coleman, Doug. "Alexandria's Civil War Ghosts & Graveyards." *Old Town Crier*, October 1, 2015. https://oldtowncrier.com.

Colgan, Chris. "Is the Olde Towne Inn in Manassas Really Haunted?" Colgan Real Estate Facebook group, October 6, 2016. https://www.facebook.com.

Colonial Ghosts. "Apparitions at Abingdon." August 15, 2017. https://www.colonialghosts.com.

———. "Colonial Williamsburg Taverns." August 15, 2017. https://colonialghosts.com.

———. "Edgewood Plantation." August 15, 2017. https://colonialghosts.com.

———. "Haunted Inns & B&Bs Outside Williamsburg." August 15, 2017. https://colonialghosts.com.

———. "Haunted Roanoke." August 15, 2017. https://colonialghosts.com.

———. "Lightfoot House—Williamsburg, Virginia." August 15, 2017. https://colonialghosts.com.

———. "The Orrell House." August 15, 2017. https://colonialghosts.com.

———. "Sleep with the Ghosts of Williamsburg." (2017). Retrieved from https://colonialghosts.com/sleep-with-ghosts-of-williamsburg

Colonial Williamsburg Hotels. "Colonial Houses Accommodations." https://www.colonialwilliamsburghotels.com.

Cooper, Rebecca. "Haunted Hotels: The Best Places in DC to See a Real Ghost over Halloween Weekend." *Washington Business Journal*, October 31, 2014. https://www.bizjournals.com/washington.

Darnell, M. Personal communication with author. March 25, 2020.

Davis, Deborah. *Some Things Go Bump in the Night: 30 Haunted Hotels, Inns, B&Bs and Restaurants.* Baltimore, MD: PublishAmerica, 2010.

Doc Halloween. "Doc Halloween Presents: Virginia Strange Sightings." March 30, 2005. http://www.members.tripod.com/dochalloween/StrangeVA.html.

Dunnlora Inn. https://www.dunnlorainn.com.

———. "Paranormal at the Dunnlora Inn." https://www.dunnlorainn.com.

———. "Welcome to the Dunnlora Inn." https://www.dunnlorainn.com.

Dye, Molly. "Four Places near Virginia Tech You Had No Idea Were Haunted." Her Campus, October 27, 2019. https://www.hercampus.com.

Edgewood Plantation. "Edgewood Plantation—A Bed & Breakfast." http://www.edgewoodplantation.com.

Emerson, L. "Charlottesville Hospitality Firm Buys Black Horse Inn." *Fauquier Now* (Warrenton, VA), 2019. https://www.fauquiernow.com.

Floyd, E. *In the Realm of Ghosts and Hauntings.* Boyne City, MI: Harbor House, 2002.

Fort Monroe. "The Fort Monroe Story." (2019). https://fortmonroe.org.

Frankenberry, Rita. "Historic Cavalier to Make Paranormal Experts Feel at Home." *Virginian Pilot* (Norfolk, VA), March 8, 2010.

Frightfind. "The Cavalier Hotel." 2019. www.frightfind.com.

Fuzzy Stone. "Haunted Places in Roanoke." Reddit. https://www.reddit.com/r/roanoke/comments/1u7oru/haunted_places_in_roanoke.

Garbitelli, Elizabeth. "Things Happen That You Can't Explain." NBC 4 Washington, October 21, 2011. https://www.nbcwashington.com.

Genuine Smithfield Va. "Mansion on Main Bed & Breakfast, A Daughter's Legacy Fulfilled." 2015. https://www.genuinesmithfieldva.com.

Ghosts of America. "Natural Bridge, Virginia Ghost Sightings." http://www.ghostsofamerica.com.

Gillard, Eric. "Boxwood Inn Haunts Up Guests with Unique Charm." *Daily Press* (Newport News, VA), November 8, 2012.

Grave Talks. "The Belle Grove Plantation: Ghost Stories, Paranormal, Supernatural, Hauntings, Horror." YouTube, April 2, 2018 (video). www.youtube.com.

Griset, Rich. "Strange Brew." *Coastal Virginia Mag*, January 21, 2015. http://www.coastalvirginiamag.com.

Gross, E. "Who Haunting Your Haunts?" *Free Lance Star* (Fredericksburg, VA), October 27, 2011. http://fredericksburg.com.

Hames, Jacqueline M. "The Haunting of Fort Monroe." U.S. Army, November 1, 2011. https://www.army.mil.

Hammel, Tyler. "Historic Albemarle Establishment Searched for Paranormal Activity." *Daily Progress* (Charlottesville, VA), February 3, 2018.

Hauck, Dennis. *Haunted Places, The National Directory: Ghostly Abodes, Sacred Sites, UFO Landings, and Other Supernatural Locations*. New York: Penguin, 2002.

Haunted Houses. "Olde Town Inn in Manassas." October 2, 2012. https://hauntedhouses.com.

Haunted Journeys. "History." 2019. www.hauntedjourneys.com.

The Haunted Places. "Haunted Room 870 at Omni Shoreham Hotel, Washington, DC." https://thehauntedplaces.com.

Haunted Places. "Wayside Inn." https://www.hauntedplaces.org.

Haunted Places to Go. "Haunted Places in Virginia: The Cavalier Hotel." https://www.haunted-places-to-go.com.

———. "Martha Washington Inn." https://www.haunted-places-to-go.com.

Haunted Rooms. "By the Side of the Road B&B, Harrisonburg, VA." https://www.hauntedrooms.com.

———. "Most Haunted Hotels in Washington, DC." https://www.hauntedrooms.com.

———. "Most Haunted Places in Virginia Beach." https://www.hauntedrooms.com.

———. "Omni Shoreham Hotel: Reported Ghosts." https://www.hauntedrooms.com.

Haunted Traveler. Jacqueline Larocca Photography. "The Haunted Hotel Monaco, Washington, DC." https://www.hauntedtraveler.com.

Haunted Travels. "The Haunted Boxwood Inn." https://www.ocoosaws.com/me/haunted-travels-usa/services/boxwood-inn-9029.html.

Hay-Adams. "The Story of the Hay-Adams." www.hayadams.com.

Heritage Media LLC. "Storefront Stories of Fredericksburg: 711 Caroline Street" (video). 2020. www.youtube.com.

Higgins, Casey. "Local History: The Hotel Roanoke in Virginia's Blue Ridge." Visit Roanoke Virginia, July 9, 2019. http://visitroanokeva.com.

Hotel Roanoke. "A Heritage of Hospitality." https://www.hotelroanoke.com.

I Go Ghost Hunting. "A Haunting We Will Go." April 14, 2008. igoghosthunting.blogspot.com.

Inn at Court Square. "About." https://www.innatcourtsquare.com.

———. "Accommodations." https://www.innatcourtsquare.com.

Jamestown, Williamsburg, Yorktown: The Official Guide to America's Historic Triangle. Winston-Salem, NC: John Blair, Publisher, 2007.

Josh. Personal communication with author. Natural Bridge Hotel, February 29, 2020.

Kelly, Gretchen. "The Linden Row Inn Keeps Edgar Allan Poe's Love Alive." *Forbes*, November 5, 2019.

Kindred Spirits. *Kindred Spirits TV Show with Amy & Adam.* Travel Channel. https://www.travelchannel.com.

Kinney, P. "The Haunted Cavalier Hotel. In The Frightening Floyds." In *Handbook for the Dead*, 1–7. Louisville, KY: Anubis Press, 2019.

———. *Paranormal Petersburg: Virginia and the Tri-Cities Area.* Atglen, PA: Schiffer Publishing, 2015.

———. *Virginia's Haunted Historic Triangle: Williamsburg, Yorktown, Jamestown, & Other Haunted Locations.* Atglen, PA: Schiffer Publishing, 2011.

———. *Virginia's Haunted Historic Triangle: Williamsburg, Yorktown, Jamestown, & Other Haunted Locations.* 2nd edition. Atglen, PA: Schiffer Publishing, 2019.

Lafayette Inn. "Meet our Feral Family." https://www.thelafayette.com.

Lamb, Scott. "The Martha Washington Inn (Haunted)." BuzzFeed, June 7, 2012. http://www.buzzfeed.com.

Lee, H. "The Martha Washington Inn's Rich Past." *Daily Press* (Newport News, VA), August 17, 2016.

Long Island Paranormal Investigators. "King's Arms Tavern." (2019). http://liparanormalinvestigators.com.

Maggie Cecilia P. (2016). "Interested in Haunted Rooms (Review)." Trip Advisor, July 24, 2016. https://www.tripadvisor.com.

Mansion Vacation Rentals. "In the Spotlight." From the *Observer, Virginian Pilot.*, February 1, 2006. https://www.mansionvacationrentals.com.

Martha Washington Inn. "The History of the Martha Washington Inn & Spa." http://www.themartha.com.

Martinez, R., and C. Trice. "Staunton Thai Restaurant Back from the Brink." Ubon Thai Victorian, October 23, 2010. http://www.ubonthaivictorian.com.

Maura. "6 Haunted Hotels Near DC That Will Make Your Stay a Nightmare." Only in Your State, August 21, 2022. https://www.onlyinyourstate.com.

McGlothlin, J. "Holiday Inn Blacksburg." Mystery 411, January 2014. http://www.mystery411.com.

Michelle. Personal communication with author. Black Horse Inn, February 22, 2020.

Molnar, D. Personal communication with author. Dunnlora Inn, October 19, 2022.

———. Personal communication with author. Martha Washington Inn, February 2, 2020.

Mystery411. "Linden Row Inn." http://www.mystery411.com.

Mystery4H. "Page House Inn." 2019. http://www.mystery4H.com.

Mystic Files. "Martha Washington Inn." http://www.mysticfiles.com.

Natural Bridge Hotel Fact Sheet. "History of the 'Grand Old Lady.'"

North Bend Plantation. "North Bend Plantation: House & Garden Tours." www.northbendplantation.com.

Northern Virginia Daily (Strasburg, VA). "Wayside Inn's Spirits Are Friendly." July 11, 2011.

Nota, A. "Richmond's Historic Linden Row Inn." *Travel Well Magazine*, February 2015. https://travelwellmagazine.com.

Nuzum, Eric. "I Ain't Afraid of No Ghost." *Washingtonian*, November 1, 2001. https://www.washingtonian.com.

Omni Hotels. "History of the Omni Homestead Resort." https://www.omnihotels.com.

———. "The Resort." https://www.omnihotels.com.

O'Rourke, John. "A Gilded and Heartbreaking Life." *BU Today*, March 13, 2012. www.bu.edu.

Parker, Stacey. "Five Things to Know about the Cavalier Hotel in Virginia Beach." *Virginian Pilot* (Norfolk, VA), March 8, 2018.

Paschall, Valerie, Michelle Goldchain and Tom Acltell. "D.C.'s 15 Most Haunted Locations, Mapped." Curbed, September 27, 2019. https://dc.curbed.com.

Poe Museum. "The Poe Museum Cats." http://www.poemuseum.org.

Polonsky, Jane Kean, and Joan Drum. *The Ghosts of Fort Monroe.* Williamsburg, VA: Polyndrum Publications, 1972.

Powell, L. "A Guide to the Ghosts and Hauntings of the American South." Southern Spirit Guide, February 5, 2018. http://www.southernspiritguide.org.

———. "The Haunts of Williamsburg, Virginia." Southern Spirit Guide, November 7, 2010. http://www.southernspiritguide.org.

———. "Orrell House: East Francis Street." November 7, 2010. http://www.southernspiritguide.org.

Regina's Haunted Library. "Haunted Places: The Jefferson Hotel," September 9, 2018 (video). YouTube. www.youtube.com.

Reinbold-Gee, S. "The Cavalier Hotel." Real Haunts, 2019. http://www.realhaunts.com.

Road Trip America. "The Chamberlin Hotel." June 26, 2005. https://www.roadtripamerica.com.

Robbins, McLean. "8 Luxuriously Haunted Hotels to Explore." Forbes Travel Guide, October 27, 2015. https://stories.forbestravelguide.com.

RVA Paranormal. "Belle Grove Plantation." November 16, 2019 (video). YouTube. www.youtube.com.

Schwartz, S. *Haunted Charlottesville and Surrounding Counties.* Atglen, PA: Schiffer Publishing, 2019.

Schwartz, T. Personal communication with author. Mansion on Main, October 21, 2018.

Shawna. Personal communication with author. Olde Towne Inn, February 22, 2020.

Shiels, Michael Patrick. "Haunted House Overnight Stay…Do You Dare?" *Forbes,* September 28, 2016.

Smith, J.J. *Haunted Alexandria & Northern Virginia.* Atglen, PA: Schiffer Publishing, 2009.

Stewart, K. "Curious Plaque Tells Forgotten Story." WTOP News, February 2, 2013. https://wtop.com.

Strock, Anna. "Here Are the 16 Weirdest Places You Can Possibly Go in Virginia." Only in Your State, October 24, 2020. https://www.onlyinyourstate.com.

———. "These Haunted Hotels in Virginia Will Make Your Stay a Nightmare." Only in Your State, August 22, 2022. https://onlyinyourstate.com.

———. "These 13 Virginia Museums Are Weird, Wacky, and Absolutely Wonderful." Only in Your State, April 2, 2015. https://www.onlyinyourstate.com.

———. "You'll Want to Cross These 22 Amazing Bridges in Virginia." Only in Your State, May 2, 2021. https://www.onlyinyourstate.com.

Taylor, L.B. *Civil War Ghosts of Virginia.* Lychburg, VA: Progress Printing Company, 1995.

———. *The Ghosts of Williamsburg, Volume II.* Lynchburg, VA: Progress Printing Company, 2004.

Things That Go Boo. "Haunted Hotels: Washington, DC." http://www.thingsthatgoboo.com.

Tipple, Stephanie. "Manassas Hotel Keeps Frightening Guest." Potomac Local News, October 2, 2012. https://potomaclocal.com.

Townsend, P. "Historic Bed and Breakfast Auctioned in Staunton." WHSV, 2010. https://www.whsv.com.

Travel Assist. "The Belle Grae Inn and Restaurant." http://www.travelassist.com.

Turkel, S. (2015). "Hotel History: The Homestead, Hot Springs, Virginia (1766)." https://www.hotelnewsresource.com/article83999.html.

Tyree, E. (2016). "Haunted or Not? Randolph College, Sweet Briar, VMI all have Reports of Hauntings." http://wset.com/news/local/haunted-or-not-randolph-college-sweet-briar-vmi-all-have-reports-of-hauntings.

Virginia Haunted Houses. "Black Horse Inn–Real Warrenton Haunted Place." https://www.virginiahauntedhouses.com.

———. "Blacksburg Holiday Inn–Blacksburg VA Real Haunted Place." https://www.virginiahauntedhouses.com.

———. "Boxwood Inn-Real Haunts in Newport News VA." (2020). https://www.virginiahauntedhouses.com/real-haunt/boxwood-inn.html

———. "The Chamberlin." https://www.virginiahauntedhouses.com.

———. "The Glencoe Inn." https://www.virginiahauntedhouses.com.

———. "Natural Bridge Hotel-Natural Bridge VA Real Haunt." https://www.virginiahauntedhouses.com.

———. "Wayside Inn–Middletown VA Real Haunted Places." https://www.virginiahauntedhouses.com.

Virginia History Museum. "Virtual Haunted Tour: The Martha Washington Hotel & Spa." October 29, 2014. https://vahistorymuseum.wordpress.com.

———. "Virtual Haunted Tour: Natural Bridge Hotel." October 17, 2014. https://vahistorymuseum.wordpress.com.

Virginia Is for Lovers. "Silver Thatch Inn." https://www.virginia.org.

Virginia Paranormal Investigations. "Belle Grae Inn: Staunton, Virginia." October 21, 2014. Facebook. https://www.facebook.com.

Washington Post. "Ghostly Shades of Poe at Linden Row in Richmond, Va." November 11, 2010.

Wayside Inn. "Wayside Inn, Since 1797." http://www.thewaysideinn1797.com.

Weir, Rachael. "Ghost Suite at the Omni Shoreham Hotel." Five Star Alliance, October 28, 2017. https://www.fivestaralliance.com.

West, R. "Ghosts and Ghouls Haunt Williamsburg's Colonial Houses." 2015. archive.makinghistorynow.com/205/10/ghosts-and-ghouls-haunt-williamsburg-colonial-houses.

Wong, S. Personal communication with author. Dunnlora Inn, July 25, 2022.

INDEX

ABOUT THE AUTHOR

Susan Schwartz, RN, MSN, MSHA, has been an avid writer for more than twenty-five years, writing about the paranormal, compiling research for freelance articles, editing manuscripts and proofing medical competencies. After publishing three short stories, she turned her attention to nonfiction, releasing *Haunted Charlottesville and Surrounding Counties* in 2019. Presently, she is a member of the Horror Writers Association and the Virginia Writers Club, where she serves as first vice-president of the state organization. She has two novels in the works: a paranormal romance and a medical thriller. In her spare time, she loves to read, travel to foreign lands and traipse through old graveyards. Please stop by and say hello at www. susanschwartzauthor.com.

FREE eBOOK OFFER

Scan the QR code below, enter your e-mail address and get our original Haunted America compilation eBook delivered straight to your inbox for free.

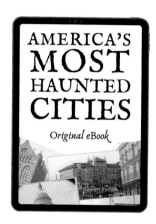

ABOUT THE BOOK

Every city, town, parish, community and school has their own paranormal history. Whether they are spirits caught in the Bardo, ancestors checking on their descendants, restless souls sending a message or simply spectral troublemakers, ghosts have been part of the human tradition from the beginning of time.

In this book, we feature a collection of stories from five of America's most haunted cities: Baltimore, Chicago, Galveston, New Orleans and Washington, D.C.

SCAN TO GET
AMERICA'S MOST HAUNTED CITIES

Having trouble scanning? Go to:
biz.arcadiapublishing.com/americas-most-haunted-cities